# *Christmas*
## *with*
# Victoria
## ~VOLUME VI~

*Text by Jennifer Cegielski*

**Oxmoor House**®

*HEARST COMMUNICATIONS, INC.*

*Christmas with* Victoria, *Volume VI*

Copyright © 2002 by Hearst Communications, Inc.,
and Oxmoor House, Inc.

*Victoria* is a trademark of Hearst Communications, Inc.

Oxmoor House, Inc.
Book Division of Southern Progress Corporation
P.O. Box 2463, Birmingham, AL 35201

ISBN: 0-8487-2530-1
ISSN: 1093-7633

Printed in Singapore
First printing 2002

We're here for you!
We at Oxmoor House are dedicated to serving you with reliable
information that expands your imagination and enriches your life.
We welcome your comments and suggestions. Please write us at:
Oxmoor House
*Christmas with* Victoria
2100 Lakeshore Drive
Birmingham, AL 35209
To order additional publications, call (205) 877-6560 or visit us at
www.oxmoorhouse.com

For *Victoria* Magazine
Editor in Chief: Margaret Kennedy
Creative Director: Cynthia Hall Searight
www.victoriamag.com

Editor: Bruce Shostak
Designer: Curtis Potter

Produced by Smallwood & Stewart, Inc., New York City

# Contents

# Foreword

Whether celebrated in a snowbound village or amid palm trees, Christmas is not about postcard perfection but about creating a little magic ⁓ magic that comes from the heart. And while holiday traditions reassure and comfort us, they also benefit from the infusion of fresh twists. As much as I cling to my own long-collected customs, I feel the need each year to tweak my decorations, wrappings, and recipes, rethinking details to keep the holiday full of surprise and wonder. As children grow up and families gather in new homesteads, celebrations evolve to reflect the changes.

To add enchantment to your own holiday, take inspiration from the enticing ideas on these pages. Many of them are cleverly simple: Tying a dozen glittery ornaments onto a chandelier multiplies the sparkle. The tiny blue beads wrapping one end of a silvered glass bulb put a keepsake spin on the ordinary. And who would guess that the crystallized gift boxes embellished with Victorian-style tags and tinsel once were humble ice-cream cartons? You can even find out where to log on to a Website to print out a dozen delightful designs for place cards, gift tags, or jam labels ⁓ I know I'll be having trouble deciding between the lacy oval and the classic swag label for my yearly yield of beach plum jelly.

At times when Christmas may seem overwhelmingly commercial, it's all these tiny, caring details that generate true spirit. May all the love you pack into your gifts and preparations enrich your Christmas with joy and peace.

*Peggy Kennedy*

EDITOR IN CHIEF, *VICTORIA*

# CHAPTER ONE

# WINTER'S COLORS

THE MAGIC OF WINTER LIES IN NATURE'S AMAZING ABILITY to decorate itself. The world seems dipped in white as snow swirls into icing-like drifts. Barren branches in the trees above revel in their icy overcoats and chime as the wind blows. Below, lush evergreens stand proud but silent, their boughs muffled with fluffy tufts of snow. The year-end sky takes on a bluish cast at twilight, and the crystalline surface of the snow

A TWILIGHT-INSPIRED
**TREASURE BOX**

SPIRALED RIBBON
**ICICLES**

WOVEN RIBBON
**STOCKING**

EMBELLISHED GLASS
**ORNAMENTS**

**SNOW AND ICE**
INDOORS

ICY **LIGHTING IDEAS**

*From its blown-glass ornaments to its treasures beneath, this tree makes the most of a frosty color palette. A few yards of fabric swathed around the base is an elegant alternative to a stiff tree skirt.*

appears to glow. As night falls, even the stars seem to shine more brightly in the heavens, like diamonds just beyond our reach.

Cozy in the warmth indoors, we watch the frost curl across the windowpanes, inviting us to join in winter's festive finery. And why not oblige? Borrow from the season's soft whites and grays, cool blues, and glittering silvers. Stockings, candles, ornaments, and wrappings all look splendid in these colors, and when brought together in quantity they create the illusion of a magical winter wonderland seemingly inhabited by old Jack Frost himself.

Collect your materials throughout the year. See a glimmering lavender box in a card shop? Snatch it up to package a Christmas gift. Spy rolls of periwinkle satin ribbon in the bargain bin at a sewing shop? Buy them, and tuck them away for holiday projects. Be on the lookout at tag sales and resale shops for silvery vintage glass ornaments ignored the rest of the year. Though all this secreting away may make you feel a bit like a magpie, you'll be grateful for your cool-hued stash when December finally arrives.

### FROST-KISSED DETAILS

*Even everyday objects share in the magic when they are colored in lovely winter-light tones. Gather candles, storage boxes, dishes, vases, and other home accents you may already have in this cool palette, or ice your holiday cookies in arctic hues and trim them with silvery candies. An unexpected item like a garden chair (opposite) set beside the tree or in an alcove offers a special place to pile presents high before Christmas. Ornaments, too, should reflect winter's palette. Thread a snowy ribbon (below) through the hanging loop of each bauble as a pretty alternative to plain wire hooks.*

*Winter's snowfall brings*
SPARKLE AND MAGIC
*to everything it touches.*

# TWILIGHT-TINTED TRIMMINGS

Wintry colored gems from the trimmings store are marvelous ingredients for dressing up all kinds of ornaments, cards and tags, and wrappings. It's hard not to be charmed by these little extras, whose sole purpose is to catch the eye. You'll have the most fun if you gather a full palette: Start with soft tones of white, dove gray, and smoke; add blues and purples such as ice, opal, aqua, lavender, and lilac; and finish with deeper colors of pewter, sapphire, and midnight accented with shimmering silver and crystal. Open a well-stocked box of trimmings, and you're sure to feel like Ali Baba finding the treasure of the Forty Thieves.

❧ A wooden box (opposite) gets new life as a trimmings safe, with old tin containers to hold the smallest bits. Think beads, baubles, buttons, braids, cording, metallic threads, appliqués, pom-poms, rickrack, and ribbon in all manner of styles from grosgrain to satin to velvet.

❧ Supplies from our cache of trimmings find a home on a handmade ornament (above). To create your own, select an array of coordinating ribbons and trims in narrow widths—include some rickracks and metallics. If you want to splurge on some extra-special trim, just buy a small supply of it and save it for the topmost piece that covers the ornament's "cap." Turn to page 129 for complete instructions.

❧ Ribbons are beautiful on their own, of course, but you might want to embellish them: Consider embroidering a seasonal message that becomes part of the bow (right), and you won't need a card.

### SPIRALED RIBBON ICICLES

*What would winter be without icicles? Our ribbon rendition (left) won't melt indoors. To make it, cut a length of narrow ribbon about 11 inches long. Next, cut a length of card stock or heavy paper, preferably with a sparkly surface, to the same width and length. Glue the two strips back-to-back with a clear-drying craft glue and, while the glue is still wet, wrap the strip in a spiral around a wooden dowel. Secure the ends of the strip in place with tape and let the glue dry overnight. Slide the icicle off the dowel, punch a hole in one end, and thread silvery cord through it to make a loop for hanging.*

### WOVEN RIBBON STOCKING

*Our satin stocking (opposite) incorporates all the colors of the winter sky. Making this charmer is easier than it looks: The ribbons are woven in an over-and-under fashion and bonded to iron-on fabric fusing. Then the weave is cut like fabric. You can use such ribbon "fabric" for other projects, too—pillows, runners, even a tree skirt.* *Turn to page 130 for instructions.*

### HOLIDAY HINT

## RECYCLING RIBBON

How often are we given a gift wrapped in gorgeous ribbon, only to discard the ribbon with the paper? Ribbons come in handy for so many holiday-season projects—why not reuse them? Though they may be creased from knots and bows, their beauty can easily be restored with a few passes of an iron. Roll the pressed lengths into coils, and hold them together with straight or safety pins until you're ready to let them delight again.

## CUSTOMIZED ORNAMENTS

*Today's plain glass ornaments are usually inexpensive and available in a wide variety of shapes and sizes. Embellish them to your liking with sparkly cording and narrow ribbon. Use a paintbrush to coat the desired portion of each ornament with glue, then wrap the trim around the ornament in a tight coil (right) or in single strands (below). For additional flourishes, glue glass beads along the ribbon or add a metallic appliqué to the top. By coordinating the baubles with your decor, you can bring holiday dazzle to chandeliers, sconces, and tabletops. A white feather tree (opposite) is the perfect open-air "curio case" for our embellished glass ornaments and ribbon icicles (see page 16). Such a tree is a charming way to brighten a corner or display an array of fragile heirloom ornaments.*

### SNOW-CHILLED GLASSES

*Wine or a cocktail often demands a chilled glass. Here's a whimsical solution—if your snowman doesn't mind sharing! Shortly before guests arrive, fill a punch bowl or large compote with fresh, clean snow (left) and gently add goblets or champagne flutes.*

### ICE-MOLD DECANTERS

*These icy-clear decanters (opposite) keep wine and vodka cold on the bar. To make one, cut off the top of a clean half-gallon milk carton and set a clear, empty bottle inside. To keep the bottle from floating, secure its mouth to the outside of the carton with masking tape. Fill the carton halfway with water, add herb sprigs, and freeze for six hours. Add more water to the carton, up to the desired level, and freeze until solid. Before serving, peel away the carton (to loosen it, run it under warm water) and fill the bottle. To absorb the inevitable drips, place the decanters on watertight trays lined with tea towels.*

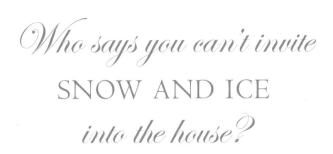

*Who says you can't invite*
SNOW AND ICE
*into the house?*

## PAPER HURRICANE LAMPS
*Paper-wrapped hurricanes (this page) cast a more intimate light than clear-glass versions. Select semitranslucent paper such as parchment or glassine. Wrap the paper casually around a tall glass votive holder. Secure the paper with a simple twist of fine-gauge wire threaded with chandelier crystals and a handful of icy glass beads.*

## CANDLE-GLOW SNOWDRIFT
*Elevated on a vintage glass cake stand (opposite), a petite snowdrift is studded with votive candles. A chilly enclosed porch would be an ideal setting for this fantasy of fire and ice. Outside, create something similar on a larger scale: Along a walkway, plant tall devotional candles into the snow.*

# CHAPTER TWO

# JOYFUL WRAPPINGS

For the true Christmas connoisseur, it's hard to decide which is more thrilling: choosing the gifts to give or selecting the ribbons and wrappings with which to adorn them. For those in favor of the latter, it's the medley of textures that entices, as crisp papers are neatly creased and lengths of glossy satins and soft velvets are measured and snipped and looped into seductive bows.

*Why limit yourself to trimming just the tree? Wrapping is an opportunity to go all out on every gift, top to bottom. Beaded garlands can stand in for ribbons, and shimmery boxes look grand when edged in tinsel.*

**LAYERED** PAPERS

RIBBON **EFFECTS**

**FLOWER** TOPPERS

HANDCRAFTED
**GIFT TAGS**

GLITTERED
**GOODIE BOXES**

BERIBBONED
**LINENS**

## LAYERED WRAPPINGS

*Every extra touch builds excitement.
Presents with party-dress allure (opposite)
get their charm from multiple elements.
Start with a wrapping of solid-color
tissue or opaque paper, then add a sheer
second covering—we used grid paper for
the gift on the left—and finish with a
woven lattice of seam binding or ribbon.
Attach a cascade of paper flowers with
dabs of glue, or let a pretty card become
the package's corsage. And what is fancy
dress without a bit of jewelry? Attach a
few ornaments that won't be easily broken,
such as these beaded wire eggs (below),
inspired by precious Fabergé creations.*

Color is sure to make a present stand out. So for a twist on Yuletide wrapping tradition, why not reinterpret the customary palette of red and green? Unexpected hues of pink and chartreuse, so fresh and festive, complement one another just as well.

To finish things off, some sparkle is essential. Tinsel garlands, metallic cording, and glitter make for glamorous accessories. Be lavish with them. And be open to offbeat ideas—raid your sewing basket, your ornament box, and your kitchen cupboards for materials. Perhaps you'll find a miniature tin cookie cutter for a baker friend or a paper flower for the gardener in your life. Handmade gift tags are also bound to make every recipient feel honored.

Once the packages have been gaily embellished, consider wrapping everyday items in your home in a bit of Christmas splendor. Napkins, runners, and tablecloths are, in a sense, wrappings for the table. They can easily be enhanced with a few whimsical details and some basic sewing skills. You'll be offering a beautiful gift: a place to share pleasurable meals with family and friends.

*The best wrappings*
INCLUDE KEEPSAKES
*to treasure long after
the papers have been
torn away.*

### ENCIRCLED GIFTS

*Sometimes a box is altogether unnecessary when wrapping unusually shaped gifts. Here, an apothecary jar filled with sweets gets a stylish tunic of vintage 1950s wrapping paper; its lid is held in place with a web of ribbons and cords. A smaller gift, rolled up in pink paper, is cinched and fringed at either end, Christmas cracker style, and finished with a neat cuff of the same vintage paper.*

## EXAGGERATED EFFECTS

*They say good things come in small packages, and we couldn't agree more. While presents may be diminutive in size (right), their wrappings can certainly have tremendous personality—this is one place where excess is fine. Why stop at just one tie? Make it three. Don't cut off that extra length of ribbon. Let it flow. And as long as you're at it, add an oversize millinery leaf or a giant gift tag for a bold flourish.*

## RIBBON RETHOUGHT

*For tying up packages, anything available by the yard is fair game. Try seam binding, dressmaker's trimmings, braided cords, yarn, or multicolored strings. On these packages (below), a length of metallic pressed-paper daisies does the trick with the help of a glue stick, and vintage green soutache is fluffed with a leftover snip of lacy pink ribbon.*

## PATTERNED TOWERS

*Multiple gifts for one lucky recipient offer an opportunity to experiment with a mix of complementary papers (above). Colors may vary, but the prints should have a similar look. Stack boxes in a tier from largest to smallest and tie up the tower with a bow.*

## FLOWER TOPPERS

*Exuberant paper and silk flowers (opposite) are cheerful reminders of warmer days ahead. They are lovely stand-ins for opulent bows on packages; let the blooms' colors inspire your choice of paper and ribbon. Attach a long stem with two small bows.*

# HANDCRAFTED GIFT TAGS

Just as a sundae seems incomplete without a cherry topper, so too does a present seem unfinished without its tag. A gift tag usually identifies the "To" and "From," but it can also announce a greeting or introduce a motif that contributes to the overall effect. And in these hurried days, it's a personal touch that actually requires little effort to make by hand. You'll find supplies to create your own gift tags at most craft and stationery stores: stickers, rubber stamps, craft punches and hole punches, and laser-printer–friendly papers. String, waxed twine, embroidery floss, or tinsel garland can all be used to attach the tags.

❧ Enhance a plain manila package tag with a layer of decorative paper to turn a vintage ornament (opposite) into a party favor or a place card. Choose a preprinted paper and use rubber alphabet stamps to add your message or a guest's name. Or design your own tag on the computer, complete with fancy fonts. Glue the paper to one side of the tag, then, using a straightedge and a utility knife, trim away the excess.

❧ Oversize craft punches turn out excellent tags. A large oval shape (above) was perfect for our "Joy" stamp. A small-diameter hole punch provided a way to fasten the tag to the box with a gossamer string.

❧ To make a button bouquet (right), select several beauties. Thread each with green paper-covered floral wire for a "stem," add millinery leaves, and tie it with ribbon inscribed with a fine-point indelible marker.

## GLITTERED GOODIE BOXES

*With a little sprucing up, ordinary paper or plastic ice cream tubs (this page) can be recycled and transformed into sparkly vintage-look containers for edible gifts like cookies or fudge. See page 132 for instructions.*

## CINCH-TOP FAVOR CONES

*Remarkably easy to make, small Victorian-style paper cones (opposite) are best suited to small gifts such as nuts or chocolates. A gently crumpled poof of tissue inserted over the contents will help keep the cinched crepe-paper top full and domed. For instructions, turn to page 131.*

With Love's Kind Greetings.

Kindest Greetings for Christmas

## "WRAPPING" THE TABLE

*Passementerie—the word has a luxurious whisper about it. Tassels, fringes, braids, and other trims (right) borrowed from the world of interior decorating can all be used to lend an eye-catching holiday edge to casual linens. Curtain tie-backs, napkins, and table runners (opposite) all join the holiday spirit in ribbon-candy shades of red and white.*

## NAPKIN TASSELS

*One has to admire the colorful intricacy of fine tassels (below). Several inches of tasseled cording are all that's required to create a playful and pretty napkin tie. Simply knot the cord around a rolled or gathered napkin.*

---

### HOLIDAY HINT

# GETTING INSPIRED

Creating a new look for your holiday table may take some experimentation. To help you select the elements, create an inspiration tray (or entire table) of china, flatware, glassware, linens, fabric swatches, ribbons, ornaments, even paint chips. Observe how they look together during the time of day you plan to entertain. Swap out items to test various combinations before deciding what to use, purchase, or make yourself.

## GUEST-TOWEL TRIMMING

*Hand towels turned out with a touch of frippery (left) are all the decorations a powder room needs. Sew on a wide jacquard ribbon for a bold regal stripe. Or tie a narrow ribbon into a prim bow before sewing it on. A matching set of towels makes a lovely handmade thank-you for a hostess.*

## RUFFLED NAPKIN RING

*With the astonishing variety of ribbons available today, you can completely coordinate your table settings. To make a generous cuff that lies flat around a neatly folded napkin (below), tack a narrow polka-dot ribbon to a wide pleated ribbon with a stitch every few inches. Cut lengths to fit the napkin, then join the ends with neat seams.*

*Fine ribbons add*
## CHARACTER
## AND COLOR
*to the simplest of linens.*

## RIBBON-EDGED TABLECLOTH

*Pretty trim breathes new life into a classic white tablecloth. Choose ribbon in a color or style that reflects those on your china, servingware, or centerpieces. A slip stitch is all you need to tack the ribbon to the cloth; this type of stitch is also easy to remove when you want to wash the tablecloth or replace the ribbon with another to coordinate with a different table setting.*

# CHAPTER THREE

# BRINGING NATURE INDOORS

Thinking of going green this season? Of course, when it comes to holiday decorations, the Christmas tree and its cousins, the wreath and the garland, are givens. Fragrant and symbolic, evergreen branches have been brought inside as part of winter festivities at least as far back as ancient Rome. These days they still symbolize enduring life and hope for a fruitful year ahead—and they offer unlimited decorating possibilities.

EXTRAVAGANT **GARLANDS**

AN INDOOR **WINTER GARDEN**

GREENERY **KEY TASSEL**

DESIGNING **CENTERPIECES**

*Why wait till the last minute? Deck the house with greenery early, creating a foundation for all your other decorations. Be lavish, and breathe in the heavenly aroma. When it's time to entertain, add fresh flowers.*

## MAGIC IN MULTIPLES

*Natural elements, repeated throughout the room, can combine with existing decor in the most exuberant or restrained ways. In a dining room (opposite), red reigns supreme, from the parade of rose and hypericum berry bouquets on the table to the bittersweet wreath on the door to the ornaments on every surface. Because a full-size tree presides in the dining room — the better for guests to enjoy it during meals — a tabletop forest of topiaries (below) in the living room has just enough presence. Pairs of wreaths on the windows show off the grand height of the architecture.*

While cut greens like pine, fir, holly, and mistletoe are traditional, a surprising number of living plants quite happily thrive indoors during the winter. Some of these beauties treat their captive audience to colorful blooms all season long, while others, like flowering bulbs, put on a limited show. There are plenty of choices to create a veritable garden in your sitting room. And don't forget the freshly cut flowers available at this time of year — when company is coming, you can adorn your rooms with striking amaryllis blooms or roses in jewel-like colors.

For another approach, turn to fruit. Simple still-life arrangements of seasonal bounty such as pears or citrus fruits — lemons, oranges, clementines, kumquats — have a painterly flair that works well for centerpieces. Place them along the length of your dining table, or pile them high in pretty compotes on a sideboard as an enticingly edible decoration. Nature's gifts of greenery, flowers, and fruit never fail to enhance our homes and remind us of how fortunate we are to have these riches at our disposal.

*Close your eyes and take in the* WONDROUS SCENT *of evergreens indoors.*

# AN INDOOR WINTER GARDEN

Though poinsettias may be an obvious Yuletide accessory, they certainly aren't the only winter plant in town. A visit to a florist or your local nursery will uncover plenty of equally—if not more—appealing options, some with attractive foliage and others with the ability to flower. Many varieties love a sunny window and will happily thrive for weeks. For an indoor show of colorful blooms, force pots of bulbs. Plan to start in late fall: look for amaryllis and hyacinths in numerous colors and for paper-white narcissus. Should you choose to force hyacinths and paper-whites, you'll also be treated to their intoxicating fragrance.

❧ Arrange a winter garden indoors (opposite) with elements you'd find in your flower beds during the warmer months. Cloches or gazing balls can mingle with the plants. Some selections here include (from left to right) wispy myrtle shaped into a tree-form topiary, aloe poised to send up a flower spike, candelabra kalanchoe with dainty trumpet-shaped flowers, and donkey's tail sedum.

❧ Holiday houseguests will be charmed by a colorful path up the stairs. Notable for their rose-shaped blossoms, hardy Rieger begonias (above) are an excellent choice for spectacular splashes of color.

❧ Blooms in pure white echo the snowy world outdoors. Potted calla lilies (right) are ideal in an east- or west-facing window; fragrant cut flowers such as freesias fill the room with their perfume.

*Fresh flowers and greenery remind us that* NATURE *is always present.*

## INSTANT FRUIT STILL LIFE

*Fabulous holiday fruit arrangements have a long tradition, but they needn't always be difficult to construct. Should you be the lucky recipient of a gift of superb fruit, put it to decorative use before it gets eaten: With little effort, a still-life grouping can be quickly designed with elements you already have— bring out a stack of cake stands (above), for example, lay out the fruit, and add a few ornaments to create a feast for the eye.*

## GREENERY KEY TASSEL

*Substitute seasonal greenery (right) for those silk tassels that grace furniture keys. Snip several bunches of seeds from a branch of seeded eucalyptus, bind them with floral wire, slip the wire through the key, and hide the wired stems with a knot of wide, luxurious ribbon. Try the same technique with boxwood or whispy white pine.*

## TABLETOP WREATH

*Wreaths don't have to hang on doors. One laid on a table makes a marvelous surround for a vase, a lamp, or a group of pillar candles. Here, kumquats dot a boxwood wreath; a Paris porcelain urn, filled with pears and more kumquats, stands at the center. Remember to safeguard your furniture with a protective layer beneath the wreath.*

## ARTFUL CENTERPIECES

*A cherished object such as a work of art is a conversation-starting focal point on a holiday table. Whatever item you choose, surround it with a mix of greenery, flowers tucked into water-filled florist's tubes, pinecones, and votive candles. This bronze head (above) is crowned with a blend that includes seeded eucalyptus and hypericum berries.*

## GARLAND FRAMES

*Be liberal as you decorate your interior architecture. Pictures, windows, doorways, banisters, and mantels all benefit from ever-green finery. A pier mirror (opposite) is framed by an impressive garland embellished with pinecones and yards of fancy ribbon; a coordinating wreath suspended from silk cord is reflected in its glass.*

# CHAPTER FOUR

# PAPER GREETINGS

Your very earliest memories of Christmas probably include paper in some way. Perhaps you recall gleefully tearing away the wrappings from a much-hoped-for gift, pasting together a chunky chain of multicolored links for the tree, or making a card for your parents once you proudly learned how to sign your name. While we may hold these childhood memories dear, we shouldn't overlook paper's more

*Christmas might be called the paper holiday. From antique molded-paper Dresden ornaments to bits of ephemera saved in albums over the years to the Internet, inspiration is everywhere.*

"DRESDEN"
**FAVOR CUPS**

WALLPAPERED
**ALBUM**

**BOOK** SLIPCOVERS

CUSTOM
**NOTES, SEALS, AND
PLACE CARDS**

sophisticated possibilities for grown-up gift-giving. Bookmarks and bookplates, greeting cards or sets of note cards, and albums are all gifts that you can easily make in the weeks leading up to Christmas.

You can tailor the gift to each person in the papers you choose. Happily, a wide range of styles is available to inspire you. Pay a visit to an art-supply store or a fine stationer to find beautiful papers from all over the world—intricate Florentine scrolls, textured Japanese rice paper, marbleized French patterns. If you're technologically savvy, you can create your own designs—replicate a favorite image from an old book or etching with a color photocopier, or use your computer to download clip-art images off the Internet, which you can then work with to make stationery on your laser printer. Though brought to life using modern techniques, the paper projects you design yourself can still have a vintage look or resemble more expensive artisan papers or letterpress styles. Your thoughtful one-of-a-kind creations are sure to be admired every bit as much as those precious childhood efforts of yesteryear.

## PAPER TRANSFORMATIONS

*A covering of durable, pretty wallpaper turns a plain scrapbook cover into a holiday gift (opposite) worthy of giving to a special friend—or keeping to collect your own Christmas memories. A small peat pot made for growing seedlings becomes a charming favor cup reminiscent of nineteenth-century cardboard Dresdens—just add paint, glitter, and a snippet from a vintage-style greeting card or tag. Little paper cups would work just as well. Turn to pages 133 and 134 for instructions.*

*Paper lets you*
CUSTOMIZE *every gift and greeting.*

## STYLISH BOOK SLIPCOVERS

*If a book is the chosen present, try this: Instead of wrapping it completely, as you would a box, make a decorative paper slipcover to conceal the publisher's book jacket or to stand in for a jacket where none exists. Cut a piece of sturdy, decorative paper large enough to wrap around the book's binding and to fold to the inside. Fold the paper around the case of the book, and tie it closed with a coordinating ribbon sash. Add a gift tag or a matching bookmark.*

THE
HOLLY
and the
FIR

## BOOKPLATE GREETINGS

*Old-fashioned black-and-white silhouette bookplates were the inspiration for our book-plate greeting (right). Photocopy the image on page 137 onto linen paper, or scan the image into your computer and print it in whatever color you wish. You can make many to use as simple greeting cards. We like using one to tuck a message into a book that, because of its value or design, is better left uninscribed.*

## MADE-TO-ORDER BOOKMARKS

*Handmade paper bookmarks (below) are the perfect accompaniments for books jacketed in the same or complementary papers, as described on the opposite page. Use the template on page 137 to cut the shape from card stock; adjust the length as desired. Trace the shape twice onto the decorative paper of your choice. Glue the paper to both sides of the card stock and allow it to dry. Make a hole at the top with a hole punch, and finish with a little tassel, knot of cord, or loop of ribbon.*

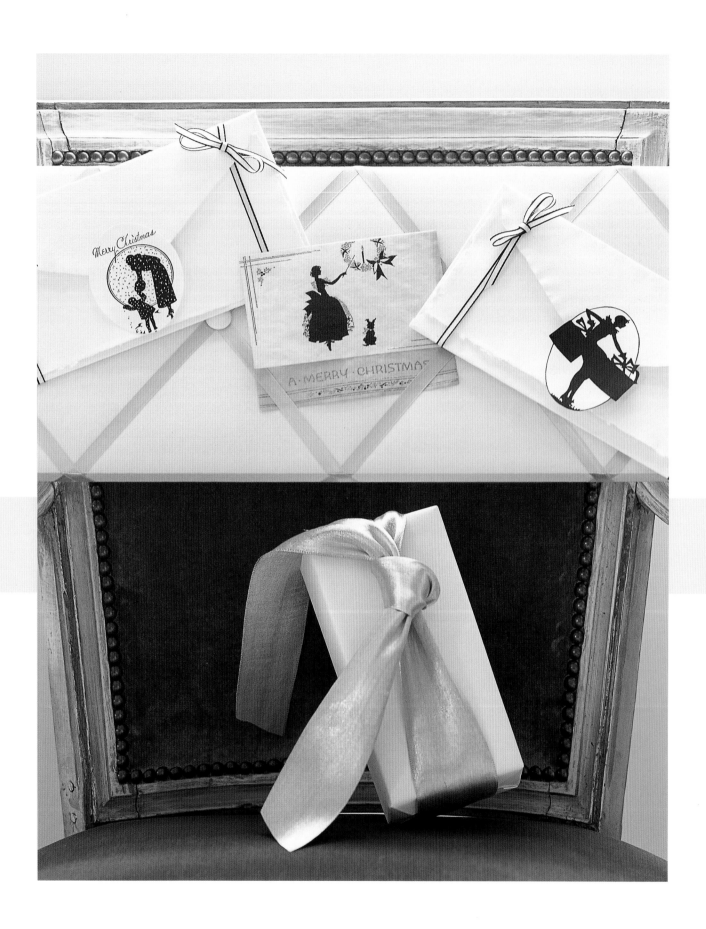

## SILHOUETTE STATIONERY

*Silhouette art dates to the late eighteenth and early nineteenth centuries, when it served as a popular alternative to more expensive painted portraits. Its quaint black-on-white imagery beautifully decorates note cards and adhesive seals (opposite). To make your own, photocopy our examples on page 137 or scan them into your computer. You can cut the images out and add a dab of glue to transform them into seals, or print out an entire series on fine-quality note cards to give as gifts.*

## BOTANICAL CARDS

*For greeting or thank-you cards with a fine printmaker feeling (above), look to botanical engravings from clip-art books or antique gardening references. Choose an image, photocopy it, and paste it onto a card. Or scan it into your computer and print enough copies on card stock to supply your holiday mailing list. If you have the computer skills, you can add words to the image or interior of the card. You can also hand-color the image with watercolors for a one-of-a-kind touch.*

## USING FOUND IMAGES

*In these projects, old meets new. Vintage images of flowers or decorative borders can be found online (see below) and downloaded into your computer to create beautiful holiday papers and lovely gifts. Once you have the images, you can modify them as you like. If you need to wrap a thin, flat gift, such as stationery, recipe cards, or photographs, a simple folded-paper portfolio (right) does the job elegantly. Decorate a card or label with one of the images, then choose good-quality card stock and cut a piece large enough to wrap your gift, plus overlap. Fold the paper around your package, secure the bundle with a piece of ribbon or cording, and tuck the card inside. Or use the images to create pretty labels for jars of preserves or to make elegant place cards (opposite). Your place cards needn't be folded or set in holders; instead, prop them against small ornaments in porcelain saucers.*

### HOLIDAY HINT

## SHARING DESIGNS

How wonderful that the Internet enables us to share information. We'd like to share this Yuletide with you. Log on to www.victoriamag.com, where you'll find colorful vintage art to use for these and other paper projects. Click on "Decorating & Projects," then on "Projects," then on "Create Decorative Place Cards, Gift Tags, & Book Plates." You'll find these and other lovely designs, as well as additional ideas and instructions.

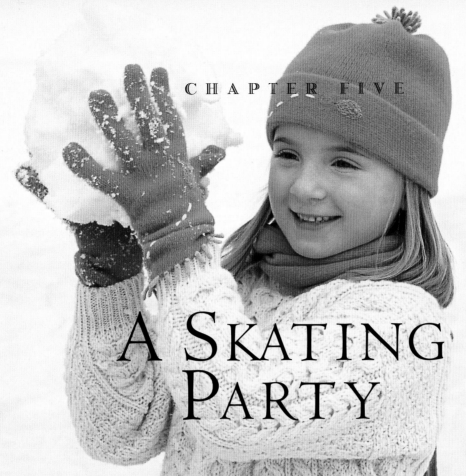

# CHAPTER FIVE

# A SKATING PARTY

SKATE **INVITATIONS**

SMOKED CHICKEN AND PUMPKIN **CHILI**

MOLASSES **CORN BREAD**

CHERRY-PECAN **OATMEAL COOKIES**

SNOWCAPPED **STRAWBERRIES**

MITTEN **FAVORS**

The sun is dazzling on the snow, the air is clear and crisp, and best of all, the temperature has been below freezing for days. You can almost hear the unmistakable scritch-scratch of skates across the ice. It's time for a skating party, so make like Hans Brinker and gather the gang for a winter frolic and a lunch outdoors. Christmas Eve morning, Boxing Day, or a chilly New Year's Day afternoon are all opportune

*Though perfect figure eights may be best left to the skilled, a skating party can be enjoyed by young and old, skaters and nonskaters alike. After all, everyone knows how to make a snowball and share a warm lunch.*

occasions for celebrating with this lively event. And even if you don't have access to a frozen pond or rink (or perhaps you don't take well to the ice), you can still share a skating-inspired afternoon at home, together with family and friends. Either way, send out handmade skate invitations and serve comforting winter fare in crowd-pleasing quantities to get in the spirit.

Rinkside, a charcoal grill is all you need to heat the tummy-warming star of the show, a bubbling pot of chili. At home, guests can cluster in the kitchen, nibbling corn bread with anticipation while the chili sends out its spicy aroma. For refreshments, stock a thermos station with plenty of mugs and hot drinks like cider, cocoa, and tea (maybe even a hot toddy or two for the grown-ups) to help chase away the cold. A garnish bar of toppings lets everyone adjust the chili to his or her taste. And when every bowl is empty, you can unveil a surprise dessert to cap the day: Replace the pot of chili with a pot of chocolate fondue, then hand out the skewers and let the sweet dipping begin.

**LACE-UP SKATE INVITATIONS**
*Miniature paper skate cards (opposite) winsomely announce the dress code (below). Make them in a variety of colors if you wish, write all the details inside—and don't forget to mention lunch! When the party's over, each card can become a souvenir ornament to decorate a Christmas tree. Turn to page 135 for instructions.*

*A day spent OUTDOORS with family and friends— who minds the cold?*

# AN OUTDOOR WINTER LUNCH

Pondside or rinkside, your lunch should build on a single-pot main dish that is convenient to carry and to heat on-site. Warming and nourishing, chili is ideal. Our version (left) combines cumin-and-cayenne spiciness with the flavors of smoked chicken and sweet pumpkin. Corn bread, the natural accompaniment, can travel to the event in the pan in which it was baked—one that turns out individual portions, like the cast-iron wedge pan we used (below), is best because the pieces can be easily served and held in the hand. In our recipe, molasses complements the sweet taste of pumpkin in the chili. Turn to pages 98 and 99 for the recipes.

🌿 She likes her chili this way, he likes his that way. A garnish bar pleases all palates: Set out small bowls of classic and creative toppings, such as grated cheddar cheese, chopped scallions, diced onions, sour cream (or plain low-fat yogurt for the health-conscious), toasted pumpkin seeds, oyster crackers. Don't forget hot sauce!

🌿 Any one-pot dish can substitute for chili and be reheated at the scene. Other suggestions for lunch: a hearty vegetable soup, a savory stew, a thick chowder, or a creamy chicken pot pie (without the crust).

🌿 A log or bench becomes an impromptu table. Set the scene with a blanket tablecloth and rustic napkins (opposite); we used denim and canvas tied with twine and decorated with pint-size pinecone tassels.

*Keep energy levels high with an assortment of* SWEETS *before the last laps around the ice.*

## TIME FOR DESSERT

*Cookies are always a crowd-pleaser with an added benefit: If it's especially chilly, you can keep your mittens on to eat them. For this party, spiced oatmeal cookies (above) get a surprise twist from tart dried cherries and pecans instead of the standard-issue raisin and walnut combination. A sip of hot cocoa (right) is a fragrant treat that warms to the toes. Offer little gingerbread men for dunking, fluffy marshmallows for floating, and rock-candy or peppermint sticks for stirring. For the grand finale (opposite), bring out skewers and a platter of plump strawberries, dried apricots, or cubes of pound cake for dipping, fondue style, into melted white chocolate; in the cold air, the candy coating hardens almost instantly. Turn to pages 99 and 100 for the strawberry and oatmeal cookie recipes.*

## LITTLE MITTEN FAVORS

*With scarves trailing and skates tossed over their shoulders (opposite), partygoers pick up a send-off surprise (this page) before heading home. To create your own version, look for toddler-size mittens or adequately sized miniature mitten ornaments. Gather squares of festive paper around candies, nuts, or trinkets, and insert the bundles into the mittens. A name tag on each favor will make every guest feel special.*

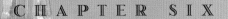

# CHAPTER SIX

# SWEET PRESENTS

Food is a gift that always delights—especially when it's the product of your own efforts. Whether unabashedly indulgent or sensibly nourishing, there's something about an edible present that is intrinsically part of the warm holiday feeling of home and hearth.

Preparing the treats on these pages does take time and energy, and that is what automatically makes them worth their weight in gold. They can be

MERINGUE
**MUSHROOMS**

**CHOCOLATE**
CONFECTIONS

SPARKLING **CAKES**

**SPICY**
CHEDDAR WAFERS

**BUTTER COOKIES** AND
**SHORTBREAD**

**CHUTNEYS** AND
**MARMALADE**

*Once you've decided on the recipes, consider matching packaging: a tall canister for a stack of cookies, a mesh bag for wrapped candies, a fancy jar for meringue mushrooms (recipe, page 101). It's a joy to be imaginative!*

appreciated by your host during a party as an additional delicacy on the sideboard, or savored in solitary pleasure after everyone has left. On the practical side, these gifts don't require batteries, always fit, and won't need to be exchanged, so they're an ideal choice for anyone on your list—especially someone whose tastes in other matters you may not know. Such gifts are also convenient for you—they can be made in advance in large batches, and identical ones can go to many different people. Part of the holiday fun may even be organizing a kitchen production line—so much fun that it might become an annual family event.

So what to make? Chocolates, candies, cookies, cakes, gingerbread, biscuits and crackers, and jams and jellies are all wonderful options. You can spoil a special someone with a favorite flavor or a secret passion, or introduce an heirloom recipe to a new friend. Presentation, of course, is the crowning touch. A paper box decorated with a festive theme or lined in colorful papers is delightful. A lasting container, with the recipe tucked inside, is even better.

## FRUIT AND NUT CLUSTERS

*Silvery corrugated boxes, tied with red ribbon and a sprig of fresh greenery (opposite), leave no doubt that treasures wait within. It's hard to imagine a more agreeable combination than the boxes' contents—bittersweet chocolate paved with delectable jewels of the season. We chose apricots, cranberries, golden raisins, and slivered almonds and pistachios for our clusters (below), but you can vary the ingredients to suit your own tastes. Turn to page 102 for the recipe.*

*Treat someone to a DELICIOUS gift— and to its recipe, too.*

## COOL CHOCOLATES

*Heart and star shapes and two kinds of chocolate make these candies (opposite) a treat for two senses. Bittersweet and white chocolate are tempered and poured into molds, then topped with a sprinkling of slightly crunchy crushed peppermint. Give the candies in a doily-lined box to a party hostess—they're a perfect after-dinner refreshment. The recipe is on page 103.*

## MARZIPAN CHERRIES

*Easily shaped by hand from marzipan and tucked into their own ruffled candy cups, these little cherry impostors (above) stand at attention, ready to be tucked into a candy box. A deep gift tin would accommodate their arching floral-wire stems (use black licorice to make edible stems). A tiny box of four, tied in ribbon, makes an amusing favor. Turn to page 104 to learn how to make them.*

## CHRISTMAS MORNING MUNCH

*The same mixture of glacéed apricots, pecans, and brown sugar is baked in layers within this moist coffee cake (above) and on top, to create its irresistibly crunchy streusel crown. Made from a classic sour-cream recipe, it will keep for up to a week and is perfect for breakfast by the tree. Nestle the cake in paper and present it in a box lined with cedar and juniper (right). The recipe is on page 105.*

## GINGERED LEMON POUND CAKE

*So beautiful when baked in a decorative cake mold or in mini-Bundt pans, this dense treat (opposite) is a ginger aficionado's dream. Three forms of ginger sparkle within, while a brushing of lemon syrup makes the exterior glisten. Turn to page 106 for the recipe.*

## ANGELIC COOKIES

*Some holiday cookies are simply just too pretty to be eaten right away. Our butter cookies (this page) are as artful as any Florentine angel. They owe their heavenly aura to a food-coloring glaze and a delicious dough shaped in an exquisite mold (see Resources). Why not make them to give as holiday tokens for special friends and colleagues? Turn to page 107 for the recipe.*

## CRANBERRY SHORTBREAD

*Packed in a container that can be enjoyed long after the treats have become a memory, sugar cookies and shortbreads make wonderful gifts for hosts. Our shortbread (opposite), baked with crystallized ginger and cranberries, is packed in an old-fashioned shortbread jar; look for similar possibilities at flea markets and tag sales. Turn to page 108 for the recipe.*

## CUPS OF CRACKERS

*Mint julep cups (opposite) are chic serving vessels for piquant cheddar sticks and rounds—cayenne pepper and sesame seeds impart extra zest. Enclose filled cups in cellophane bags for a gracious gift wrap. The spicy wafer recipe is on page 109.*

## GOOD-FOR-YOU GOODIES

*For a sensible snack that will appease the diet gods but indulge a friend, toss together your own custom-blended trail mix (right). No recipe required: Choose any combination of nuts and dried fruit. Almonds, cashews, pistachios, cherries, cranberries, blueberries, raisins—the choices, and proportions, can be tailored to your friend's tastes. Natural touches such as raffia and pinecones keep the wrapping in the spirit of the contents.*

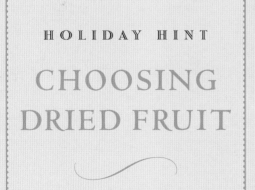

HOLIDAY HINT

# CHOOSING DRIED FRUIT

The holidays and dried fruit have a long shared history, dating to the early English tradition of the Christmas pudding. Fruitcake still dominates, yet dried and glacéed fruits are delicious on their own and in other recipes. Raisins, figs, dates, prunes, and apricots are confirmed favorites, but almost any fruit is available dried. Plump and colorful blueberries, strawberries, cranberries, mangoes, and peaches can all flavor your holiday treats.

### FRUITY CHUTNEYS

*A piquant condiment, chutney is of Indian origin. British colonialists adapted it to their own tastes, and these flavorful cooked versions (left) trickled down into English cuisine. Serve them with grilled or roasted meats or over vegetables. Chutney can be made in large batches and packaged in Mason jars, which makes it a natural for holiday gift-giving. The recipes are on page 110.*

### READY-TO-SERVE WRAPPING

*Sometimes a hostess's gift of food is intended to be served right at the party. To make things easy, carry your contribution in a reusable container complete with a serving spoon (below). Even a simple lidded glass bowl can look festive—just add a dapper oversize ribbon to keep the lid secure, and stow the serving spoon in the knot.*

*Simple, sophisticated,*
SUBLIME *~a pot of*
*jam or relish*
*from your own kitchen.*

## MARMALADE FAVORS

*After a brunch, invite guests to take home their own supply of this orangy confection—its unique sweetness comes from the addition of dried Australian apricots, which are meatier than most. We tied squares of pretty gold paper around each lid and piled the jars high on a triple-tiered pastry stand; you could set a jar, decorated with a name tag, at each place setting instead. The recipe is on page 111.*

# CHAPTER SEVEN

# HOLIDAY ENTERTAINING

**SAVORY** HORS D'OEUVRES

ROASTED **PUMPKIN SOUP**

CIDER-GLAZED **ROAST TURKEY**

**CHOCOLATE** PECAN PIE

**APPLE AND CRANBERRY** TART

**FLAVORFUL COOKIES**

he house is dressed in its holiday finery and everyone's in the Christmas spirit. So extend an invitation to friends. There are many ways to entertain, whether you're expecting a group of six or a crowd of sixty. Events can be formal or informal, intricately planned or impromptu. There's always a classic sit-down dinner, or you might choose to host an open house with finger foods, an evening buffet with stations

*Set the scene with silver, linens, candles, and flowers. Is it cocktails for a crowd? A few friends for tea? A traditional dinner? Whatever you decide, serve delicious seasonal fare and bring out your holiday best.*

of both sweet and savory options, or a tea and caroling party. On the following pages are foods that work for any kind of party.

For a large buffet, prepare simple fare that is self-serve or bite-size. Save more complicated hors d'oeuvres, such as our pecan-crusted chèvre tartlets or Parmesan-lime crisps, for when you're hosting a group of six to ten. For a sit-down meal, set the table with your best wares and take full advantage of our turkey-dinner menu. A tree-trimming party might end with tea and our Madeira cake and ginger-lime and bourbon-currant cookies.

Whatever the nature of your holiday party, use candles everywhere to bathe your rooms in a welcoming glow; glass hurricanes and votives will shelter flames in crowded, active rooms. Mass plenty of fresh-cut flowers simply; winter whites such as narcissus and amaryllis are good choices. Jazzy classics or Christmas instrumentals always make for lively musical accompaniments, but keep the volume low so as not to overpower conversation. Good friends, good food, good cheer ⁓ is there any better way to celebrate?

## WINTER WHITES

*It's snowing outside, so why not serve a mix of hors d'oeuvres all in white? A table is set up in the main entry hall (opposite), with platters of crispy fennel, endive, cauliflower, and cucumber crudités. Such white cheeses as farmhouse Cheddar, Caerphilly, and goat cheeses fit the bill. Even sweets can join in on the snowy theme: Meringue cookies and a miniature white cake (below) complement the lush amaryllis centerpiece.*

*Christmas parties are the perfect time to* RECONNECT *with old friends.*

## SAVORY HORS D'OEUVRES

*By hosting a small gathering, you'll have an opportunity to make a selection of little bites that might be too complicated and time-consuming to prepare by yourself for a large party. Let guests fill their own plates, tapas style, and choose from (opposite, clockwise from top left) pecan-crusted tartlets filled with chèvre, skewered chicken with mango chutney, and crunchy Parmesan-lime crisps with pine nuts. The recipes for all three hors d'oeuvres are on pages 112–114.*

## GRILLED CHEDDAR LEAVES

*Finger foods should look enticing. Toasted Cheddar cheese sandwiches (right) become party fare with the help of a leaf-shaped cookie cutter. Sage leaves hidden within add a sophisticated, unexpected flavor. Turn to page 115 for the recipe.*

## TWO-BITE SANDWICHES

*Open-face sandwiches (left) borrowed from teatime are easy to assemble for a crowd. Cut slices of firm bread into small squares or triangles, or use miniature slices, then top with an assortment of your favorite fillings— try our curried chicken or diced carrots with vanilla. The recipes are on pages 114 and 115.*

# A ROASTED DINNER

For the most elegant, comforting sit-down feast, consider this all-roasted dinner. Start with roasted pumpkin soup (left); for ease during the holiday bustle, this recipe can be made a day or two ahead. A proper turkey (opposite) is a classic; our version gets a twist with a tangy cider glaze and a flavorful stuffing of dried apples, sausage, and toasted pecans. A wintry root-vegetable side dish (below) mixes sweet and white potatoes, carrots, and parsnips; roasting brings out their natural sweetness. A gingered cranberry sauce cleanses the palate. Include our chive and Cheddar corn sticks and sautéed green beans to complete the menu. The recipes are on pages 116–120.

🌿 Thanksgiving Day, Christmas Eve or Day, New Years Eve or Day—the holiday season is undeniably the right time for a full-scale sit-down dinner. It's the perfect time to put your vintage serveware to good use. Fearlessly mix and match china and flatware, and bring out special pieces like grand soup tureens, covered vegetable dishes, platters, and decanters for a wonderfully, eclectically dressed table.

🌿 When the turkey is the centerpiece, introduce flowers on the table in a different way. Create an individual arrangement for each guest with a few blooms tucked into a julep cup or a small antique vessel.

🌿 Instead of using a traditional white tablecloth, create a base of deep, rich color. Don't invest in a new tablecloth; instead, purchase yardage of a wide fabric, cut right off the bolt, and hem or fringe the two raw ends.

### APPLE TART WITH CHEDDAR

*We love the sweet-and-savory combination of this dessert (left). The apples' tartness works well with the tanginess of the Cheddar; use Gala or Golden Delicious apples for the best flavor. The edges of the crust are folded for a rustic look. The recipe is on page 123.*

### MADEIRA CAKE

*A generous slice of Madeira cake (below) is a pleasing finish with an after-dinner drink. Grated lemon peel within and candied orange peel on top provide its citrusy zing. This is a versatile dessert, good at any time of day; try it for brunch, afternoon tea, or a midnight snack. For the recipe, turn to page 124.*

### PIE OR TART FIRST?

*A dessert buffet (opposite) encourages everyone to head back for seconds. In the foreground: The pastry crust of a traditional pecan pie gets a twist with cocoa powder. On the cake stand: The apple-cranberry tart blends cornmeal and hazelnuts in the crust for a toothsome crunch. The table is dressed with colorful and fragrant garnishes— mint and scented geranium leaves bring a subtle scent, while green gooseberries and golden cape gooseberries glisten like jewels. The recipes are on pages 121 and 122.*

## MOLASSES CRINKLES

*These bite-size cookies (left) boast all the aromatic spices of the holidays—cinnamon, ginger, and clove. With their dusting of granulated sugar, they sparkle in candlelight. Their diminutive size makes them ideal for farewell favors: Wrap up a few for each guest to carry home in a pocket. Turn to page 125 for the recipe.*

## GOOD-NIGHT TEA AND COOKIES

*Those few friends who linger for more conversation after an evening buffet will enjoy a warming cup of tea before they head out into the cold. Some comforting cookies (opposite) end the night with a concentration of flavor: ginger-lime for the rounds and bourbon-currant for the squares. Turn to pages 126 and 127 for the recipes.*

Turn to page 125 for the recipe.

Turn to pages 126 and 127 for the recipes.

### HOLIDAY HINT

# ENDING WITH TEA

Tea is a soothing finish to an evening of revelry. Here's how to brew the best pot: Always boil fresh water; filtered is best. Measure one teaspoon of tea per cup, and add one more for the pot. Though you'll want to brew all teas to taste, most blends should be steeped for at least three minutes but no longer than five. To keep it hot longer, warm the pot with boiling water or hot tap water, then empty it out before brewing the tea.

# Recipes

The recipes in this section are listed below alphabetically for easy reference. The page number
for the recipe is given first; the page number for the photograph is given second, in italics.

# smoked chicken and pumpkin chili

3 tablespoons olive oil or vegetable oil

2 onions, chopped

1½ to 2 tablespoons chili powder, or to taste

1 teaspoon ground cumin

Salt to taste

½ teaspoon cayenne pepper, or to taste

2 red or yellow bell peppers, diced

3 cloves garlic, minced

4 cups cubed pumpkin or butternut squash (about 2 pounds)

1 teaspoon dried oregano

2 boneless, skinless smoked chicken breasts (about 1½ pounds), cut into ½-inch pieces

2 cups canned diced tomatoes

2 cups canned crushed tomatoes

2 cups cooked or canned drained chickpeas

2 cups cooked or canned drained white beans

Toasted pumpkin seeds, yogurt, sour cream, shredded Cheddar cheese, and sliced scallion, for garnish (optional)

*There's something about chili that just seems intrinsically warming. Maybe it's the tingling flavor of the chilies, maybe it's the fact that this crowd-pleasing one-dish meal is such a favorite choice for casual, festive gatherings. This soulful version blends the distinctive taste of smoked chicken with that wonderfully reliable fall and winter ingredient: pumpkin. It's a most convenient dish to prepare for any event because you can make it a day in advance — the flavors will be even better by the time you reheat and serve it.*

1. In a large saucepan or casserole, heat the oil. Add the onions and cook over medium heat, stirring occasionally, for 5 minutes, or until soft. Add the chili powder, cumin, salt, and cayenne pepper, and cook, stirring occasionally, for 5 minutes more. Add the peppers and garlic and cook, stirring occasionally, for 5 minutes. Add the pumpkin and oregano, toss to combine, and cook, stirring occasionally, for 5 minutes more.

2. Add the smoked chicken, diced tomatoes, and crushed tomatoes and simmer, stirring occasionally, for 15 minutes. Add the chickpeas and the beans and simmer for an additional 5 to 10 minutes, or until heated through. Serve with desired garnishes.

# ✣ m o l a s s e s   c o r n   b r e a d ✣

1 cup yellow cornmeal

1 cup all-purpose flour

2 teaspoons baking powder

1½ teaspoons ground coriander

½ teaspoon salt

¼ teaspoon cayenne pepper, or to taste

2 large eggs, lightly beaten

4 tablespoons unsalted butter, melted

1 cup buttermilk

2 tablespoons molasses

*Molasses gives this quick bread a sweetness that complements our Smoked Chicken and Pumpkin Chili. For a hearth-and-home holiday feeling, we like to bake it Southern style in a cast-iron skillet, but you can use a baking dish or cast-iron corn-bread molds if you prefer; simply adjust the baking time accordingly.*

1. Preheat the oven to 425°F.

2. Liberally oil an 8- or 9-inch cast-iron skillet and place it in the oven to preheat for 5 minutes.

3. In a bowl, combine the cornmeal, flour, baking powder, coriander, salt, and cayenne pepper. In another bowl, beat together the eggs, butter, buttermilk, and molasses. Add the egg mixture to the dry ingredients and stir until just combined.

4. Pour batter into the heated skillet and bake for 15 to 20 minutes, or until a cake tester inserted in the center comes out clean. Serve warm or cooled.

# ✣ s n o w c a p p e d   s t r a w b e r r i e s ✣

YIELD: 8 SERVINGS

12 ounces white chocolate, broken
      into small pieces

2 tablespoons vegetable shortening

1 quart fresh strawberries

*Do any flavors complement each other better than chocolate and fresh strawberries? In this recipe, the berries get a winter-white coating. Because they're served whole, select the most glorious berries you can find. If chunks of best-quality white chocolate are unavailable, use packaged white chocolate chips.*

1. In a double boiler, melt the chocolate with the shortening, stirring frequently. Remove the pan from the heat and let the chocolate cool for a few minutes.

2. Skewer the strawberries on fondue forks or wooden skewers and dip into melted chocolate at an angle so that a portion of each berry remains uncoated. The strawberries may be eaten as soon as they are coated, or they may be placed on a tray lined with waxed paper and cooled. They are best served within a few hours.

# cherry-pecan oatmeal cookies

YIELD: ABOUT 4 DOZEN COOKIES

1¾ cups all-purpose flour

½ teaspoon baking soda

1 teaspoon baking powder

½ teaspoon cinnamon

½ teaspoon freshly grated nutmeg

¼ teaspoon salt

1 cup unsalted butter, softened

1¼ cups firmly packed dark-brown sugar

½ cup granulated sugar

2 large eggs, lightly beaten

2 teaspoons vanilla extract

2½ cups old-fashioned rolled oats

¾ cup toasted pecans, chopped

¾ cup dried cherries, chopped

*At a prim and proper party, artful and delicate holiday cookies are sheer heaven, to be sure, but what can top a big, chewy oatmeal cookie after a kitchen lunch or an afternoon party of skating and sledding? Old-fashioned rolled oats guarantee that these will have just the right ratio of coarse crumb to moist texture. Toasted pecans give them a hint of nuttiness, and dried cherries are a pleasantly sweet-tart alternative to the more traditional raisins. Slip individual cookies into waxed-paper sleeves and line them up in a basket. Guests will enjoy carrying them away in their pockets for a nibble later in the afternoon.*

1. Preheat the oven to 350°F.

2. In a bowl, whisk together the flour, baking soda, baking powder, spices, and salt until combined.

3. In the bowl of an electric mixer, using the paddle attachment if available, cream the butter with the sugars until the mixture is light and smooth. Add the eggs and vanilla and beat to combine. Stir in the flour mixture just to incorporate. Stir in the oats, pecans, and cherries.

4. Drop the batter by large, rounded tablespoons onto ungreased cookie sheets, leaving about 2 inches between cookies. Flatten the cookies slightly with a spatula before baking. For best results, bake the cookies one sheet at a time, in the upper portion of the oven, for 8 to 10 minutes, or until lightly browned. Let the cookies cool on the baking sheets for 2 to 3 minutes, then transfer them to racks to cool completely. Store the cookies in airtight containers.

# ✤ meringue mushrooms ✤

3/4 cup sugar

3 large egg whites, at room temperature

1/8 teaspoon salt

1/8 teaspoon cream of tartar

1/2 teaspoon vanilla

Sifted confectioners' sugar

About 2/3 cup melted chocolate or
    1 recipe Chocolate Ganache
    (recipe follows)

Sifted unsweetened Dutch-process
    cocoa powder

1. In a heavy saucepan over medium heat, combine the sugar and 1/4 cup water and bring to a simmer, swirling the pan and washing down the sides of the pan with a brush dipped in cold water, until the sugar is dissolved. Boil the syrup, undisturbed, until a candy thermometer registers 240°F (soft-ball stage).

2. In the meantime, in the bowl of an electric mixer, beat the egg whites with the salt until foamy. Add the cream of tartar and beat the whites until they form soft peaks. With the mixer running, add the sugar syrup in a stream, and continue beating the meringue for 8 minutes, or until cool. Beat in the vanilla.

3. Preheat the oven to 200°F. Line one or two baking sheets with parchment paper.

4. Transfer meringue to a pastry bag fitted with a 1/4-inch plain tip. Pipe 40 small mounds onto the paper, each about 1 inch in diameter, to create mushroom caps. Then, holding the pastry bag straight up, pipe 40 cones onto the baking sheet, to create mushroom stems. Dust the caps and the stems with confectioners' sugar and bake for 2 hours, or until they are completely dry.

5. Make mushrooms in one of two ways: For mushrooms that will last up to two weeks in airtight containers, dip a stem tip into melted chocolate and make a mushroom by pushing the chocolate-covered tip into the bottom of a cap. Let dry. For mushrooms filled with Chocolate Ganache, which will last up to one week if kept refrigerated in tightly covered containers: After 1 1/2 hours of baking time, remove the sheet (or sheets) from the oven and gently push in the undersides of the mushroom caps. Return to the oven and bake for 30 minutes more. Turn off heat, and let stand in the oven overnight. Transfer the Chocolate Ganache to a pastry bag fitted with a 1/4-inch fluted tip, and pipe the cream into the undersides of the caps to simulate gills. Push a stem into each cap and chill until the ganache is firm.

6. Before serving, lightly dust the mushrooms with sifted cocoa powder.

# ❧ chocolate ganache ❧

YIELD: ABOUT 1¼ CUPS

½ cup heavy cream

6 ounces semisweet chocolate, chopped

*This rich, indulgent chocolate icing should be a standby in every baking and candy-making repertoire. You can use it to glaze cakes, pastries, and tortes. Here, we use it to assemble our Meringue Mushrooms (recipe on previous page).*

Have the chocolate ready in a bowl. In a small saucepan over medium heat, bring the cream just to a simmer. Immediately pour the hot cream over the chocolate and stir until the mixture is melted and smooth. Chill the ganache just until it is firm enough to pipe.

# ❧ fruit and nut clusters ❧

YIELD: ABOUT 18 CANDIES

½ pound bittersweet chocolate, tempered (instructions on the opposite page)

½ cup combination of dried fruits and nuts, such as dried pieces of apricot, cranberries, golden raisins, roasted and salted or unsalted cashews, almonds, pistachios, and hazelnuts

*A cross between a healthful snack and a decadent sweet, these irresistible little rounds are chock-full of three stalwarts of the season: nuts, dried fruits, and chocolate. You can vary the mix of nuts and fruits to suit your taste; the bittersweet chocolate will be the perfect foil for any combination. Try some clusters with cashews only, some with a trio of nuts, others with only fruit. You might use diced candied orange peel for a fragrant addition. And we can never repeat it too many times: It's Christmas, so buy the very finest chocolate you can find, such as Valrhona or Callebaut. Packed in a waxed-paper–lined box or holiday tin, these homemade confections may just be this year's gift of choice for chocolate lovers. Chances are you'll soon find yourself making this recipe over and over — be sure to make a batch for yourself, too.*

1. Line a baking sheet with parchment paper. Using a tablespoon, drop the tempered chocolate onto the paper, holding the spoon about 2 inches above the paper and letting the chocolate drip off the spoon. It will form natural rounds. Top each round with some of the dried fruits and nuts.
2. Place the baking sheet in the refrigerator and chill the clusters for 30 minutes, or until hardened. Store the clusters between sheets of parchment or waxed paper in a cool, dry place.

# ✦ chocolate peppermint bites ✦

YIELD: ABOUT 2 DOZEN CANDIES

**6 ounces bittersweet chocolate, tempered (instructions follow)**

**6 ounces white chocolate, tempered (instructions follow)**

**1 cup crushed peppermint candy**

*These delicious candies are sure to please even the most sophisticated palates. Look for chocolate molds at baking-supply stores. And, as always, choose top-quality chocolate; it will make all the difference.*

1. Temper the dark chocolate. Pour a very thin layer of the dark chocolate into each mold. Let cool for 10 minutes.
2. Temper the white chocolate. Pour a very thin layer of white chocolate over the dark chocolate. Sprinkle with peppermint. Chill until set.

# ✦ tempering chocolate ✦

*Tempering, which results in a chemical and physical change in the chocolate, is the process of raising, lowering, and raising again the temperature of melted chocolate. Chocolate in "poor temper" will look dull or gray, or streaked, or have a coarse, granular texture when broken up. Tempered chocolate has a beautifully glossy, crisp texture and will keep longer than untempered chocolate, making it essential for the two preceding chocolate-candy recipes. Use a candy thermometer to check the temperature regularly. Stir the chocolate to make sure your reading is accurate, and hold the thermometer in the chocolate, not resting on the bottom of the pan, which will be hotter. There are several methods for tempering, but the following technique is the most widely used. Be forewarned: It can be quite messy.*

1. Break the chocolate into 1-inch pieces or smaller. In the top of a double boiler set over simmering water, melt the chocolate, stirring frequently with a clean, dry spatula, until it registers about 120°F (but no hotter) on a candy thermometer. Remove the double boiler from the heat.
2. Pour two thirds of the chocolate onto a cool, clean, dry surface, such as marble or Formica. With a palette knife, smear the chocolate evenly across the work surface, going back and forth over the chocolate. Bring the chocolate together with a scraper, and use the palette knife to clean the scraper. Repeat the spreading and scraping process, working quickly to prevent lumps from forming, and mixing the chocolate evenly. Check the temperature of the chocolate; when it reaches 80° to 82°F and takes on a dull, matte look, return it to the chocolate in the double boiler. (Depending on the temperature of the kitchen, this process will take anywhere from 5 to 20 minutes of continuous work.)
3. Stir gently and constantly with a rubber spatula, trying not to create air bubbles, until the chocolate is smooth. Take the temperature of the chocolate; it should read 84° to 91°F (dark chocolate should be 86° to 91°F, milk and white chocolate 84° to 86°F). If the chocolate is above 93°F, you will have to begin tempering again from scratch; if it falls below this range, return the pan to the heat to further heat the chocolate.

# ⚘ marzipan cherries ⚘

YIELD: ABOUT 3 DOZEN CHERRIES

**1 pound marzipan paste at room temperature**

**Red liquid food coloring**

**Thin black licorice laces**

*This time of year, marzipan fruits may not grow on every tree, but they do seem to appear in every confectioner's counter and gourmet market. Some shapes and coloring demand a higher level of expertise, but this harvest of cherries is an easy project for marzipan beginners. Look for plastic-wrapped logs of marzipan — a mixture of almond paste, sugar, and egg whites — in supermarkets and specialty food stores. And skip the proverbial bowl for these cherries: Fluted white-paper candy cups are the ideal cradles for these creations. For more realistic stems, cut short lengths of floral wire to insert into the cherries' stem ends in Step 1. Cherries made this way are more suitable for decorative display, of course, but if they are to be eaten, be sure to remove the wires beforehand.*

1. Marzipan dries out quickly, so keep it tightly covered in plastic and work with only one piece at a time. Pinch off a small piece of marzipan, about enough to form a 1-inch ball. Roll the ball between the palms of your hands (wiping them occasionally with a damp cloth to prevent sticking), to shape the marzipan into a natural cherry shape. Using the pointed end of a bamboo skewer, gently make an indentation at the stem end, pull it out, then roll the skewer down the side of the cherry, pressing gently, to simulate the fruit's cleft. Push a short length of licorice into the hole at the stem end to form a stem. Let the marzipan cherries dry, uncovered, on sheets of foil or waxed paper overnight.

2. With a soft, clean watercolor brush dipped in the food coloring, tint the cherries to the desired hue of red; this may take several applications. Allow them to dry in between applications. Let the cherries dry on waxed paper or foil, uncovered, for 1 day. They will keep, refrigerated, in an airtight container for up to 8 weeks.

# ❧ apricot-pecan coffee cake ❧

YIELD: 1 CAKE

## FOR THE FILLING AND STREUSEL TOPPING

¼ cup firmly packed light-brown sugar

¼ cup granulated sugar

1 cup toasted pecans

2 teaspoons cinnamon

½ teaspoon salt

¼ teaspoon freshly grated nutmeg

½ cup finely diced Australian glacéed apricots or similar dried apricots, plus 5 dried apricots, for garnish

½ cup cake flour

6 tablespoons unsalted butter, cut into bits

½ teaspoon pure vanilla extract

## FOR THE BATTER

2 cups cake flour

1½ teaspoons baking powder

½ teaspoon baking soda

½ teaspoon salt

1½ sticks unsalted butter, softened

1 cup sugar

2 large eggs, lightly beaten

1½ teaspoons vanilla

1 cup sour cream

## FOR THE GARNISH

Confectioners' sugar

*Don't let the name deceive you—yes, coffee cake is peerless with coffee, but it's also good for a simple breakfast, a satisfying snack, or a mealtime dessert, especially with a scoop of vanilla or pecan ice cream at its side. If you've been invited to be a houseguest during the holidays, bring one along; chances are you'll be invited back next Christmas. In this recipe, the apricot in the filling and streusel topping add a refreshing bit of tang.*

1. Preheat the oven to 350°F. Butter and flour a 9-inch springform pan.

2. Make the filling and topping: In a food processor, combine the sugars, pecans, cinnamon, salt, and nutmeg. Process until the nuts are coarsely ground. For the filling, place ¼ cup of the nut mixture in a bowl and stir in the apricots, making sure they do not clump. Set aside. To the remaining topping, add the flour, butter, and vanilla. Process till crumbly. Transfer to a bowl.

3. Make the batter: Sift the flour, baking powder, baking soda, and salt into a bowl. In the bowl of an electric mixer, cream the butter. Add the sugar a little at a time and beat until light and fluffy. Add the eggs slowly. Add the vanilla. Alternately beat in the flour mixture and the sour cream, starting and ending with flour.

4. Transfer a third of the batter to the pan and sprinkle with half the apricot filling. Add half the remaining batter and sprinkle with the remaining filling. Add the rest of the batter. Distribute the topping evenly over the batter.

5. Bake for 50 to 60 minutes, or until a cake tester inserted in the center comes out clean. Let cool in the pan. Remove the sides of the pan and transfer the cake to a serving dish. Arrange whole apricots in the center of the top of the cake. Before serving, dust with confectioners' sugar. The cake will keep, wrapped in plastic, for up to 1 week.

# gingered lemon pound cake

YIELD: 1 CAKE

FOR THE BATTER

2 cups flour

1 teaspoon baking powder

1/2 teaspoon ground ginger

1/2 teaspoon salt

1 cup (2 sticks) unsalted butter

1 cup sugar

4 large eggs, lightly beaten

2 teaspoons pure vanilla extract

2 tablespoons peeled and minced fresh ginger

1/4 cup milk

1/4 cup crystallized ginger, minced (optional)

FOR THE LEMON SYRUP

1/3 cup freshly squeezed lemon juice

1/3 cup sugar

*If you like lemon pound cake and you like gingerbread, you'll love this recipe. The cake gets its intense flavor from three kinds of ginger in the batter: ground, fresh, and crystallized (candied). It makes such a pretty gift when it's been baked in a decorative mold, so do use one if you have it — or be on the lookout for a new or vintage version that suits your fancy. If you want to make several little cakes in individual serving molds, adjust the baking time accordingly. A jar of your favorite chocolate or fruit topping would be a delicious partner with a gift of this moist cake.*

1. Preheat the oven to 325°F. Butter and flour an 8-cup decorative mold or a loaf pan.

2. Into a bowl, sift the flour, baking powder, ground ginger, and salt.

3. In the bowl of an electric mixer, cream the butter. Add the sugar, a little at a time, and beat until light and fluffy. Beat in the eggs, one at a time, and the vanilla and the fresh ginger. Beat in a third of the flour mixture and half the milk. Repeat with half the remaining flour mixture and all of the remaining milk. Add the remaining flour mixture, beating until just combined. Fold in the crystallized ginger, if desired. Pour the batter into the prepared pan and smooth the top. Bake for 50 to 60 minutes, or until a cake tester inserted in the center comes out clean.

4. Meanwhile, make the lemon syrup: In a small saucepan, combine the sugar and the lemon juice and heat, stirring, until the sugar is dissolved.

5. Invert the cake onto a rack and, while it is still hot, gently brush the top and sides with the lemon syrup. Let it cool completely. The cake will keep, wrapped tightly in plastic, for up to 1 week.

# ✢ a n g e l  b u t t e r  c o o k i e s ✢

YIELD: ABOUT 8 COOKIES

FOR THE COOKIES

1 cup (2 sticks) unsalted butter, softened

1¼ cups sugar

1 large egg, lightly beaten

1½ teaspoons vanilla extract

4 cups all-purpose flour, plus extra
    for dusting mold

Pinch of salt

Vegetable oil

FOR THE GLAZE (OPTIONAL)

1 cup confectioners' sugar

Liquid food coloring

*Note: Follow this recipe to make cookies like those pictured on page 78. To do so, you will need the angel mold listed on page 142 in Resources. You can use the dough from this recipe to make simple shapes and leave them unadorned; the cookies will be just as delicious.*

1. In the bowl of an electric mixer, cream the butter and sugar until fluffy. Beat in the egg and vanilla. In another bowl, sift together the flour and salt. Slowly add the dry ingredients to the butter mixture, beating until just combined. Do not overmix. Form the dough into a disk, wrap it in plastic, and chill it for 5 hours or overnight.

2. Chill the angel mold, then lightly brush it with vegetable oil, coating all crevices and indentations. Wipe away excess oil with paper towels. Sift flour over the mold, tipping it back and forth, until it is evenly coated. Hold the mold upside down and lightly tap it against a surface to remove excess flour. Flour the mold before making each cookie, but do not re-oil.

3. Break off a piece of chilled dough large enough to fit into the mold. (Leave the remaining dough in the refrigerator.) Gently knead the dough in your hand two or three times to smooth out wrinkles, and press it quickly into the mold while it is still cold and slightly stiff. When the mold is completely filled, press the dough to remove air pockets and form an even cookie. Carefully press any dough extending over the edges back inside the form. The cookie should not be thicker than the mold. Use a large knife to trim the dough flush with the edge of the mold.

4. To unmold the cookie, rap the edge of the form repeatedly against a wooden board, rotating the mold at the same time. When the cookie is loosened all over, tap or gently peel it out onto a baking sheet. If the dough sticks to the mold, carefully loosen it with the point of a paring knife. Prepare the remaining cookies in the same manner, spacing them 2 inches apart on the cookie sheet. Chill the cookies.

5. Preheat the oven to 350°F. Bake the cookies for 8 to 11 minutes, or until lightly golden around the edges. Let them cool on the sheet for 5 minutes, or until firm enough to handle. With a wide spatula, transfer them to wire racks and let cool. The cookies can be eaten plain or glazed.

6. To glaze the cookies: In a small bowl, combine confectioners' sugar with enough water to form a glaze. Divide the glaze among small bowls and tint with food coloring. Cookies can be brushed with a single glaze or painted with different colors, using paintbrushes in different sizes.

# cranberry shortbread

YIELD: 2 DOZEN COOKIES

1 cup (2 sticks) unsalted butter, softened

½ cup superfine sugar

2 cups all-purpose flour

¼ cup cornstarch

¼ teaspoon salt

⅔ cup coarsely chopped dried cranberries

¼ cup minced crystallized ginger

*Scottish tradition holds that the notched edges ringing a round of shortbread represent the sun's rays. What could be a better gift of hope and joy this time of year? As a substitute for the more predictable currants or candied orange peel, dried cranberries provide a decidedly Yankee twist to this classic Scottish dish. Serve it as a whole wheel, and give everyone the pleasure of snapping off a triangle.*

1. Line one large or two small baking sheets (to accommodate three 6-inch rounds) with parchment paper.

2. In the bowl of an electric mixer, cream the butter and sugar until light. With the mixer on low, add the dry ingredients slowly. Add the cranberries and ginger, mixing just until crumbly. Transfer the dough to a lightly floured surface. Gently knead until it just comes together. Divide the dough into three balls and transfer them to baking sheets, pressing each into a round about 6 inches in diameter. With a large sharp knife, cut each round into eight wedges. Do not pull sections apart. With a small knife, score the edges of each round to create a scalloped edge. With the tines of a fork, decoratively score the top of the dough. Chill for at least 15 minutes.

3. Preheat the oven to 350°F.

4. Bake the shortbread for 25 to 30 minutes, or until the edges are lightly browned. Let cool for 15 minutes, then transfer to racks to cool completely. The shortbread can be cut into wedges while warm or kept in rounds to be cut or broken apart at serving time.

# spicy cheddar wafers

YIELD: ABOUT 2 DOZEN WAFERS
OR 1 DOZEN LOGS

6 ounces sharp Cheddar cheese, grated

6 tablespoons unsalted butter, cut into bits

2/3 cup all-purpose flour

1/2 teaspoon salt

1/8 teaspoon cayenne pepper, or to taste

1 egg yolk

Egg wash made by beating 1 egg white with
    1 teaspoon water and a pinch of salt

3 tablespoons black sesame seeds, or a
    combination of black and white
    sesame seeds

*In the spirit of good cheer, neighbors visit one another around Christmas—sometimes unexpectedly. It's nice to have something on hand to carry with you as a tasty token, or to share with visitors to your own house. Flecked with sesame seeds, these savory biscuits go well with a glass of wine, a bit of cheese, and some olives. The versatile dough can be shaped into wafers or logs; once they've cooled, divide them into gift containers—small boxes, flea-market jars, simple beakers, or pretty bowls, perhaps—that will protect them from breaking. Add a wrapping of cellophane or tissue as needed, finish with a length of ribbon or cord, and you're all set to go.*

1. In a food processor, combine the cheese, butter, flour, salt, and cayenne. Process with an on-off action until the mixture is combined. Add the egg yolk and process until the mixture just comes together in a ball.

2. Preheat the oven to 375°F. Line baking sheets with parchment paper. Pinch off 1-inch pieces of the dough, roll between your palms to form balls, and flatten balls to 1/4 inch thick. Arrange rounds 2 inches apart on baking sheets. Brush the tops with egg wash and sprinkle with sesame seeds. Bake for 12 to 15 minutes, or until crisp and golden.

3. Alternatively, pinch off 2-inch pieces of the dough, roll between your palms to form 6- to 7-inch logs, and transfer to baking sheets. Brush the tops with egg wash and sprinkle with sesame seeds. Bake for 12 to 15 minutes, or until crisp and golden.

4. Cool on the sheets for 5 minutes, then transfer to racks to cool completely. Store in airtight containers for up to 1 week.

# piquant apricot chutney

YIELD: ABOUT 5 CUPS

2 cups dried apricots, chopped

1 cup dates, pitted and coarsely chopped

1 cup brown sugar, firmly packed

1 cup sugar, or adjusted to taste

1 cup cider vinegar

1 small onion, chopped

1 tablespoon peeled and minced fresh ginger

2 small dried red chilies, seeds removed, crushed

Juice of 1 lime

1 clove garlic, finely minced

*This amber-colored chutney, made with dried apricots and dates and sparked by red chilies, has a zesty sweet-and-sour flavor that makes it a wonderful condiment with roasted meat, poultry, or vegetables. A small bowl of it on a cocktail tray set with breads and cheeses gives guests a chance to experiment with flavor combinations. Refrigerated in a sealed jar, the chutney will keep for about a month.*

1. In a bowl, pour just enough boiling water over the apricots and dates to cover them. Let the fruit "plump" for at least 2 hours or overnight.

2. In a 4-quart stainless-steel pot, combine the sugars, vinegar, onion, ginger, chilies, lime juice, garlic, and 1¼ cups water. Bring to a boil, then reduce heat and simmer, uncovered, until the mixture thickens, about 20 minutes.

3. Drain the apricots and dates, and stir them into the simmering mixture. Continue cooking at a simmer for 15 to 20 minutes more, until the fruit softens. Cool, pour into jars, and seal.

# apple chili chutney

YIELD: ABOUT 4 CUPS

2½ pounds cooking apples, peeled, cored, and finely chopped

1⅓ cups brown sugar

2 cups malt or cider vinegar

1 small onion, finely chopped

2 cloves garlic, minced

1 small piece of ginger (about 1½ inches long), peeled and finely grated

½ cup currants

½ teaspoon mustard seed

4 green chilies, de-seeded and finely chopped

*Served cold or slightly heated, this mild chutney is a perfect accompaniment to cold meats and game, making it a thoughtful gift for a holiday-party hostess. Increase the garlic or ginger for added spiciness. Stored for at least two weeks before serving, its flavor will mellow and improve. Refrigerated in a sealed jar, the chutney will keep for about a month; write or print out that information on a tag or label if you're giving it as a gift.*

In a 4-quart stainless-steel pot, bring apples, brown sugar, and vinegar to a simmer and cook over medium heat until the apples are soft, about 15 minutes. Add the onion, garlic, ginger, currants, mustard seed, and chilies. Simmer, uncovered, until the chutney is thick and pulpy, about 20 minutes. Cool, pour into jars, and seal.

# ⚜ orange marmalade ⚜
## with dried apricots

YIELD: ABOUT 4 HALF-PINTS

3 large Valencia or navel oranges

1 large lemon

3 to 4 cups sugar

1/2 pound dried apricots, diced

*We can raise our crust of marmalade-spread toast in appreciation to the Scots, who invented this citrusy jam back in the late 1700s as a way to preserve the rare, fresh fruit. For this recipe, seedless navel oranges or extra-tangy Valencia varieties are best. Marmalade makes a good holiday production-line favor or gift: Fold a square of decorative paper or printed fabric over the lid of each jar and cinch it with ribbon or cord. When it's time to distribute the gifts, just tie on little name tags.*

1. Remove the peel from the oranges and the lemon, being careful not to include the white pith. Cut the peel into slivers. Remove the pith from the oranges and the lemon. Halve each, and remove and discard the seeds. Cut the fruit into dice, being careful to reserve the juice, and transfer to a large heavy casserole or kettle. Add 3 cups water and simmer, uncovered, for 10 minutes. Cool and let stand, covered, overnight.

2. Measure the fruit mixture. For every cup, add a scant 1 cup sugar. Return to the casserole and bring to a boil, stirring, until the sugar is dissolved. Boil gently, stirring occasionally, for 25 minutes. Stir in the apricots, return to a boil, and boil for 10 to 15 minutes more, or until a candy thermometer registers 218° to 220°F. Skim off the froth, stir for 1 minute, and ladle into sterilized 1/2-pint jars, filling to within 1/8 inch of the tops. Wipe off the rims and seal the jars. Cool, check the seals, and label, including the date. Store in a cool, dark, dry place. Marmalade keeps for about 3 months.

# pecan tartlets with chèvre

YIELD: 28 TARTLETS

One 15-ounce package pie crust

⅓ cup pecans, coarsely ground

1 tablespoon extra virgin olive oil

3 small onions, thinly sliced

Salt and freshly ground pepper to taste

1 teaspoon sugar

22 ounces chèvre (goat cheese) at room
temperature, crumbled

½ cup pitted black olives, chopped

*Pecans give the crusts of these savory little tarts a touch of sweetness that subtly balances the sautéed onions, chèvre, and black olives. Served warm from the oven on a cold winter's eve, they'll be instantly devoured, so you may want to bake them in two or three batches. Sherry is an ideal drink to serve with them.*

1. Preheat the oven to 350°F.

2. Unfold the pie crust rounds on a sheet of waxed paper and spread the ground pecans over each round. Press the pecans into the dough using a rolling pin. Cut the dough into rounds to fit 28 small tartlet pans, about 3 inches in diameter, and press into the pans. With a fork, pierce the dough. Line the dough with rounds of parchment or foil and weight with rice. Bake for 15 minutes, or until lightly browned. Remove paper and weights and cool to room temperature.

3. In a large skillet, heat the oil over moderate heat. Add the onions and salt and pepper and cook, stirring occasionally, until softened, about 5 minutes. Sprinkle the sugar over the onions and cook, stirring, until golden brown.

4. Transfer the onions to a bowl, add the chèvre and olives, and stir until combined well. Divide the filling among the shells and bake on a baking sheet for 10 minutes or more, or until the cheese is heated through. Serve immediately.

# ☙ skewered chicken ☙
# with mango chutney

YIELD: 40 APPETIZERS AND ABOUT
1½ CUPS OF CHUTNEY

## FOR THE SKEWERED CHICKEN

6 slices firm-textured white bread

1 tablespoon dried garlic flakes

1 large egg

1 teaspoon Dijon mustard

4 boneless, skinless chicken breast halves,
    each cut into 10 bite-size pieces

Vegetable oil for frying

## FOR THE MANGO CHUTNEY

2 large firm-ripe mangoes, peeled and
    cut into chunks

Juice of 1 lime

¼ teaspoon red pepper flakes

*The most interesting finger foods for a cocktail party mingle a variety of flavors and textures. Skewered meats are common in many cultures, but the mango-chutney dipping sauce in this recipe gives the chicken an Indian flair. If you want to provide a trio of chutneys for more dipping options, include bowls of our Piquant Apricot Chutney and Apple Chili Chutney (recipes on page 110).*

1. In a food processor, combine the bread and garlic flakes and process until the bread is light and fluffy. Transfer the crumbs to a shallow plate. In a bowl, whisk the egg and mustard until smooth. Dip the chicken into the egg mixture, letting the excess drip off, and dredge in the bread crumbs.

2. In a large skillet or saucepan over medium heat, add enough oil to measure 1½ inches and heat it to 300°F. Add the chicken in batches and cook, stirring occasionally, until crisp and golden. Transfer to a plate lined with paper towels to drain. Pierce each piece of chicken with a wooden skewer and arrange on a serving plate.

3. Make the mango chutney: In a food processor, combine all ingredients and process until smooth. Transfer to a serving bowl.

# ✤ parmesan-lime crisps ✤
## with pine nuts

YIELD: ABOUT 24 CRISPS

12 ounces coarsely grated Parmesan cheese

Grated zest of 1 lime

⅓ cup pine nuts, coarsely chopped

1. Preheat the oven to 300°F. Line a baking sheet with parchment paper or foil and brush lightly with oil.

2. In a bowl, mix together the grated cheese and lime zest. Drop the mixture by spoonfuls about 2 inches apart onto the baking sheet and sprinkle with some of the nuts. Bake for 10 to 15 minutes, or until the cheese is bubbly and melted. Let stand 5 minutes before removing to a rack to cool completely. Repeat with the remaining mixture.

# ✤ curried chicken tea sandwiches ✤

YIELD: 4 TO 6 SERVINGS

¼ cup finely diced pineapple

¼ cup mayonnaise

1 tablespoon Dijon mustard

¾ teaspoon curry powder, or to taste

Salt to taste

2 cups finely diced cooked chicken

¼ cup finely diced celery

2 tablespoons minced scallion

¼ cup slivered almonds

¼ cup golden raisins, soaked in hot water for 10 minutes and drained

¼ cup each quartered red and green seedless grapes

1 tablespoon snipped fresh dill

6 slices firm-textured bread, crusts removed

*This type of sandwich is adapted from traditional afternoon tea fare. Several tastes and textures contribute to its flavor: piquant curry and fragrant dill, crunchy celery and almonds, and sweet additions of pineapple, raisins, and grapes. The filling, delicious for full-size sandwiches, is especially good for two-bite open-face sandwiches for cocktails.*

1. In a bowl, combine the pineapple, mayonnaise, mustard, curry powder, and salt.

2. In another bowl, toss together the chicken, celery, scallion, almonds, raisins, grapes, and dill. Add the mayonnaise mixture and stir gently to combine. Let stand, covered, for 30 minutes to allow the flavors to develop. Spread the mixture on bread and cut the bread into quarters.

# grilled cheddar leaves

YIELD: 16 HORS D'OEUVRES

8 thin slices "lite" wheat or white bread

8 slices white Cheddar cheese

1 bunch fresh sage leaves

4 tablespoons unsalted butter

1. Arrange the bread on a work surface. Cover half the slices with a slice of cheese, top the cheese with a few sage leaves, and cover the leaves with the remaining cheese. Top with the remaining bread, forming four sandwiches. Using a small leaf-shaped cookie cutter, cut four leaves out of every sandwich. Or remove the crusts from each sandwich and halve it twice diagonally, forming four triangles.

2. In a large nonstick skillet over medium heat, melt half the butter. Add half the sandwiches and grill on each side until the bread is golden and the cheese is melted through. Transfer to a serving plate and grill the remaining sandwiches the same way.

# carrot-vanilla tea sandwiches

YIELD: 4 TO 6 SERVINGS

1 cup sugar

2 cups finely diced carrot

1/3 cup orange juice

1 tablespoon vegetable oil

1 tablespoon Oriental sesame oil

2 teaspoons grated orange rind

Seeds from a 1-inch piece vanilla bean

1/2 teaspoon grated fresh ginger

1/4 cup golden raisins, soaked in hot water for 10 minutes and drained

1/2 teaspoon minced candied ginger

1 tablespoon minced fresh mint

Salt to taste

8 slices firm-textured brown bread

2 tablespoons black sesame seeds

*The sweet and savory flavors in this carrot-based filling are heightened by the aromatic magic of vanilla bean seeds. Do use a dense brown bread— its fuller flavor and sweetness is the tastiest platform for this unusual mixture.*

1. In a saucepan, combine 3 cups water and the sugar and bring the mixture to a boil, stirring occasionally, until the sugar is dissolved. Add the carrots and cook over medium-high heat for 5 minutes. Drain the carrots and refresh under cold water. Drain and pat dry.

2. In a bowl, whisk together the orange juice, vegetable oil, sesame oil, orange zest, seeds from the vanilla bean, and the fresh ginger. Add the carrots, raisins, candied ginger, mint, and salt to taste and toss to coat. With a slotted spoon, arrange the mixture on the brown bread and garnish with the black sesame seeds. Cut into quarters.

# roasted pumpkin soup

YIELD: 8 SERVINGS

FOR THE SOUP

One 4- to 5-pound sugar pumpkin or similar
    pumpkin, quartered and seeded

2 tablespoons unsalted butter

1 large onion, minced

2 celery stalks, thinly sliced

3 large garlic cloves, minced

6 to 7 cups homemade chicken stock or
    canned low-sodium chicken broth

1 tablespoon minced fresh sage leaves, or
    1 teaspoon dried, crumbled

1 sprig fresh thyme, or 1 teaspoon dried,
    crumbled

1 bay leaf

Salt and freshly ground pepper to taste

FOR THE SAGE CREAM

1 cup crème fraîche or sour cream

1 tablespoon finely minced fresh sage leaves,
    or to taste

Salt and freshly ground pepper to taste

FOR THE GARNISH

Vegetable oil for frying

16 large fresh sage leaves

*Throughout the autumn and winter, having a great soup recipe on hand is essential. This seasonal soup is exceptionally versatile: Serve it as a first course for a formal dinner or as a casual lunch with grilled-cheese sandwiches. It can be prepared a day ahead, covered, and refrigerated; to serve, just reheat and add the delicious flourish of our sage cream and crisp, translucent fried sage leaves.*

1. Preheat the oven to 400°F. Lightly oil a baking sheet.

2. Place the pumpkin pieces, cut sides down, on the baking sheet and roast for 25 to 30 minutes, or until tender when pierced with a fork. Let cool, then scoop out the flesh. Discard the shells.

3. Meanwhile, in a large saucepan, melt the butter over medium heat. Add the onion, celery, and garlic, and cook, stirring occasionally, for 5 to 7 minutes, or until the onion is lightly golden. Add 6 cups of the stock, the sage, thyme, bay leaf, salt and pepper, and simmer for 20 minutes. Add the pumpkin to the stock mixture and simmer for 15 minutes. Discard the thyme sprig and bay leaf.

4. In a food processor, puree the soup in batches. Return the puree to the saucepan. If it is too thick, thin with the remaining stock. Heat the soup and adjust the seasoning.

5. Make the sage cream: In a bowl, combine all ingredients.

6. Make the garnish: In a small skillet, heat 2 inches of vegetable oil to 350°F. Fry the sage leaves in small batches, stirring gently, for 15 to 20 seconds, or until translucent. With a slotted spoon, transfer the leaves to a plate lined with paper towels to drain.

7. To serve, ladle the soup into bowls or soup plates. Top each serving with a dollop of the sage cream, and garnish with two sage leaves.

# cider-glazed roast turkey

YIELD: 8 TO 10 SERVINGS

FOR THE TURKEY

One 16- to 18-pound fresh turkey

Salt and freshly ground pepper to taste

1 recipe Dried Apple, Sausage, and Toasted
    Pecan Stuffing (recipe follows)

1/2 cup (1 stick) unsalted butter, softened

2 cups unsweetened apple cider

2 cups canned low-sodium chicken broth

Lady apples, Seckle pears, fresh figs, grapes,
    and/or fresh herbs for garnish (optional)

FOR THE GRAVY

1/3 cup all-purpose flour

3 cups homemade turkey stock or chicken
    stock, or canned low-sodium chicken
    broth, heated

1 tablespoon tomato paste, or to taste

1 bay leaf

1 large sprig fresh thyme or
    1 teaspoon dried, crumbled

1 large sprig fresh rosemary or 1 teaspoon
    dried, crumbled

Worcestershire sauce to taste (optional)

Freshly squeezed lemon juice to taste

Salt and freshly ground pepper to taste

1. Preheat oven to 325°F. Remove and reserve turkey neck and giblets for stock. Rinse the turkey and pat dry. Season cavities with salt and pepper. Stuff neck cavity loosely with some of the stuffing, fold neck skin under bird, and fasten with a skewer. Loosely stuff the body cavity. Spoon remaining stuffing into a buttered baking dish, cover with foil, and chill.

2. Truss the turkey. Rub it with half the butter and season with salt and pepper. Arrange, breast side up, on a rack in a large roasting pan. In a saucepan over medium heat, melt the remaining 1/4 stick of butter in 1 cup of the cider. Cut a double layer of cheesecloth large enough to cover the turkey breast entirely, rinse it in water, and squeeze dry. Soak the cheesecloth in the cider/butter mixture and arrange it over the breast. In a large measuring cup, combine the remaining cider with the chicken broth. Cover the breast with foil. Pour 2 cups of the cider-stock mixture into bottom of roasting pan and roast the turkey. Baste every 1/2 hour with juices, lifting the foil to baste the breast. Add the remaining cider-stock mixture to the pan as liquid evaporates. Roast until a meat thermometer inserted in the thickest part of the thigh reads 180°F, about 4 1/2 hours. Remove foil and cheesecloth during the last hour to allow skin to brown.

3. Transfer the turkey to a large platter, cover loosely with foil, and let it rest for at least 20 minutes. Increase oven to 425°F. Bake stuffing in the baking dish, covered with foil, for 30 minutes, or until heated through.

4. Make the gravy: Pour the drippings from the roasting pan into a large measuring cup. Skim fat from surface, reserving both. Place roasting pan on two burners over low heat. Add 1/4 cup of reserved fat and whisk in the flour; cook, whisking, until golden brown. Add the stock in a stream, whisking; add reserved drippings. Add tomato paste, bay leaf, thyme, and rosemary. Bring to a boil. Reduce heat to low; simmer, stirring occasionally, for 20 minutes, or until slightly thickened. Season with Worcestershire sauce, lemon juice, and salt and pepper. Strain into a sauceboat.

5. Remove the strings from the turkey and transfer it to a serving platter. Garnish with fruit and fresh herbs. Carve, and serve with additional stuffing and the gravy on the side.

# dried apple, sausage, and toasted pecan stuffing

YIELD: ABOUT 12 CUPS

1 pound sweet Italian sausage, removed from casings

6 tablespoons unsalted butter

3 cups minced onion

2 cups finely diced celery

4 garlic cloves, minced

8 to 10 cups toasted or dried cubed (1/2-inch) good-quality bread

1 1/2 cups chopped toasted pecans

1 cup chopped dried apples

1/2 cup minced fresh parsley

1 tablespoon minced fresh thyme, or 1 1/2 teaspoons dried, crumbled

1 tablespoon minced fresh sage, or 2 teaspoons dried, crumbled

Salt and freshly ground pepper to taste

1 to 2 cups turkey stock or canned low-sodium chicken broth

*While it's impossible to know who first had the brilliant idea of stuffing a bird with a savory bread side dish before roasting, everyone now enjoys this tradition wholeheartedly. Many families may have generations-old recipes they lovingly make again and again, year after year. But when you're ready to try something new, consider this flavorful version. Made with sausage, toasted pecans, and dried apples, it's truly the perfect complement to our Cider-Glazed Roast Turkey (recipe on previous page).*

1. In a large, deep skillet, cook the sausage over medium heat, stirring, for 5 minutes, until it is no longer pink. With a slotted spoon, transfer the sausage to a large bowl. Discard the fat remaining in the skillet.

2. Melt the butter in the skillet over medium heat. Add the onions, celery, and garlic, and cook, covered, over medium-low heat, stirring occasionally, for 5 to 7 minutes, or until the vegetables are soft. Scrape the vegetables into the bowl with the sausage and stir. Add the remaining stuffing ingredients except the stock and toss to combine well. Add enough stock to moisten the stuffing slightly. The stuffing may be made a day ahead, covered, and refrigerated until ready to use.

# ⚘ roasted root vegetables ⚘

YIELD: 8 SERVINGS

4 carrots, cut diagonally into ½-inch slices

4 parsnips, cut diagonally into ½-inch slices

2 Idaho potatoes, peeled and cut into
    ½-inch dice

2 sweet potatoes, peeled and cut into
    1-inch dice

3 to 4 tablespoons olive oil, or to taste

1 to 2 tablespoons minced fresh rosemary, or
    1 to 2 teaspoons dried, crumbled

Salt and freshly ground pepper to taste

2 tablespoons softened unsalted butter,
    or to taste

¼ cup minced fresh parsley leaves, or to taste

*Slow-roasting root vegetables brings out their subtle flavors. This colorful combination of carrots, parsnips, white potatoes, and sweet potatoes is both salty and sweet. If you like this dish, you might want to experiment by adding other roast-worthy vegetables, such as turnips, butternut squash, or beets, to the mix.*

Preheat the oven to 425°F. In a large bowl, toss the vegetables with the oil, rosemary, and salt and pepper. Arrange the vegetables on a large baking sheet in one layer. Roast for 30 to 35 minutes, turning occasionally, or until golden and tender. Transfer the vegetables to a serving dish and toss with butter and parsley.

# ⚘ gingered cranberry sauce ⚘

YIELD: 8 SERVINGS

1½ cups sugar

1 cup ruby port or dry red wine

1 tablespoon peeled and minced fresh ginger

Two 12-ounce packages fresh cranberries

⅛ to ¼ teaspoon ground cloves, or to taste

1 stick cinnamon

One 10-ounce jar wild lingonberries in sugar,
    available at specialty food stores

⅓ to ½ cup crystallized ginger, minced

*Ginger has been a popular sweetmeat as far back as the Middle Ages. Spicy and aromatic—indeed one of the quintessential tastes of Christmas—it raises cranberry sauce to a zesty new level. This recipe calls for two types: fresh and crystallized (or candied).*

1. In a saucepan over medium heat, combine the sugar, port or wine, and fresh ginger, and bring to a boil, stirring. Add the cranberries, cloves, and cinnamon, and simmer the mixture, stirring occasionally, until it is thickened, about 10 minutes.

2. Stir in the lingonberries and crystallized ginger and transfer to a dish. Let cool, cover, and chill for 6 hours, or overnight. Remove the cinnamon stick and transfer the sauce to a serving dish.

# chive and cheddar corn sticks

YIELD: 10 CORN STICKS

1 cup ground cornmeal

1 cup all-purpose flour

2 tablespoons sugar, if desired

1 teaspoon salt

2 teaspoons baking powder

1/2 teaspoon baking soda

1 cup buttermilk

2 large eggs

1/2 stick unsalted butter, melted

1 cup grated Cheddar cheese

1/4 cup chives

*Instead of a basket of rolls on the dinner table, try a plate stacked with irresistible corn sticks. Here, they're gussied up with chives and Cheddar cheese. You'll need two corn-stick molds, which are widely available from kitchen-supply stores and catalogs.*

1. Preheat the oven to 400°F.

2. Heat two corn-stick molds in the oven until hot.

3. Into a bowl, sift the cornmeal, flour, sugar, salt, baking powder, and baking soda. In a small bowl, whisk together the buttermilk, eggs, and butter. Add the milk mixture to the cornmeal mixture and stir just until moistened.

4. Gently stir in the cheese and chives.

5. Brush the hot corn-stick molds with vegetable shortening or butter and spoon the batter into the molds. Bake for 15 minutes, or until golden. Invert onto racks to cool.

# sautéed green beans with shallots and dill

YIELD: 8 SERVINGS

2 pounds green beans, trimmed

2 tablespoons olive oil

1/2 cup minced shallots

Salt and pepper to taste

1 to 2 tablespoons snipped fresh dill

1 teaspoon grated lemon peel

2 to 3 teaspoons freshly squeezed lemon juice, or to taste

1. Have ready an ice-water bath. In a saucepan of boiling salted water, blanch the green beans for 6 to 7 minutes, or until just tender. Drain the beans and transfer them to the ice-water bath to stop the cooking and set their color. Drain the beans and pat them dry. The beans, up to this point, may be prepared one day in advance; if doing so, transfer them to a plastic storage bag and refrigerate.

2. In a large skillet over medium heat, cook the shallots in the olive oil, stirring occasionally, until lightly golden. Add the green beans and salt and pepper and cook, stirring, until heated through. Add the dill, lemon peel, and lemon juice, toss to coat, and transfer to a serving dish.

# chocolate pecan pie

YIELD: 8 SERVINGS

FOR THE CHOCOLATE PASTRY DOUGH

1½ cups all-purpose flour

⅓ cup unsweetened cocoa powder,
    such as Dutch-process

½ cup confectioners' sugar

¼ teaspoon salt

½ cup (1 stick) unsalted butter, cold,
    cut into bits

2 tablespoons vegetable shortening, cold

1 large egg, lightly beaten

½ teaspoon vanilla, or to taste

FOR THE FILLING

1 cup dark corn syrup

½ cup sugar

⅛ teaspoon salt

4 tablespoons unsalted butter, melted

3 large eggs

2 tablespoons dark rum

1 teaspoon vanilla

2 cups toasted pecan halves

Vanilla ice cream or lightly whipped cream,
    for serving (optional)

*Traditionally a staple of Southern kitchens, pecan pie is a sublimely chewy and intensely sweet dessert. With the addition of cocoa to the pie crust, this version furthers the pie's candy-like reputation. A bit of rum deepens the rich flavor of the filling. If you're serving other desserts with this one, some guests may ask for only a very thin slice, so a single pie may yield more servings than expected.*

1. Make the chocolate pastry dough: Into a bowl, sift the flour, cocoa powder, sugar, and salt. With a pastry cutter, cut in the cold butter and vegetable shortening until the mixture resembles coarse meal. Add the egg and vanilla, and stir until the dough is formed. Flatten the dough into a disk and chill, wrapped in plastic, for 30 minutes. Roll out the dough between sheets of lightly floured waxed paper to fit about an inch beyond the rim of a 9-inch pie pan. Fit the dough into the pan and fold the edge to a double thickness, trimming and shaping as needed for a rounded finish. To create a twisted-rope effect as pictured on page 92, gently score diagonal lines along the rim with the side of a bamboo skewer. Lightly prick the shell with the tines of a fork, and chill for 20 minutes.

2. Preheat the oven to 350°F. Place a baking sheet in the lower third of the oven to heat.

3. Make the filling: In a saucepan, combine the corn syrup, sugar, and salt, and bring to a boil. Remove the saucepan from the heat and add the butter. In a bowl, whisk the eggs, rum, and vanilla. Add the syrup/butter mixture and whisk to combine.

4. Arrange the pecans concentrically on the crust. Skim any foam from the filling and discard. Carefully pour the filling over the pecans. With the back of a spoon, press the pecans down so that they are covered by the syrup. Transfer the pie pan to the baking sheet in the oven and bake for 45 minutes. Cool on a rack. Serve warm or at room temperature with vanilla ice cream or lightly whipped cream, if desired.

# apple and dried cranberry tart

FOR THE CRUST

½ cup stone-ground cornmeal

½ cup all-purpose flour

½ cup finely chopped toasted hazelnuts

⅓ cup light-brown sugar

½ teaspoon ground cinnamon

½ teaspoon salt

¼ teaspoon freshly grated nutmeg

6 tablespoons unsalted butter, melted

FOR THE FILLING

¼ cup sugar, or to taste

2 tablespoons unsalted butter, melted

1 teaspoon grated lemon peel

1 tablespoon freshly squeezed lemon juice

½ teaspoon ground cinnamon

½ pound Golden Delicious apples, peeled,
    cored, and cut into ¼-inch slices

1 tablespoon all-purpose flour

½ cup dried cranberries, or to taste

FOR THE GLAZE

½ cup apricot preserves, sieved

1 tablespoon Calvados, Armagnac, or Cognac
    (optional)

*For a wonderfully apple-infused meal, prepare this tart as the finale to a main course of Cider-Glazed Roast Turkey with Dried Apple, Sausage, and Toasted Pecan Stuffing (recipes on pages 117 and 118). You can serve it warm or at room temperature, perhaps with a small dollop of ice cream or crème fraîche.*

1. Make the crust: In a food processor, blend the cornmeal, flour, nuts, sugar, cinnamon, salt, and nutmeg. Pulse to combine. Add the butter and pulse until the mixture is evenly moist and looks crumbly. Transfer the mixture to a 9-inch tart pan. With your fingertips or the back of a large spoon, distribute the crumb mixture over the bottom and sides of the pan, gently pressing it into place. Make sure the coating is even. Chill the crust while preparing the filling.

2. Preheat the oven to 400°F. Heat a baking sheet in the lower third of the oven.

3. Make the filling: In a bowl, stir together the sugar, butter, lemon peel, lemon juice, and cinnamon. Add the apples, sprinkle with the flour, and toss to combine. Arrange the apples concentrically in the tart shell. Sprinkle the cranberries over the apples. Transfer the tart to the baking sheet in the oven and bake for 35 minutes, or until the apples are tender and the top is golden. Cover the tart with foil if it begins to brown too much.

4. Make the glaze: In a small saucepan over medium heat, combine the apricot preserves and Calvados (or 1 tablespoon water) and cook, stirring, for 4 minutes, or until syrupy. Brush the glaze over the tart. Serve warm or at room temperature.

# apple tart with cheddar

YIELD: 6 SERVINGS

FOR THE DOUGH

1¼ cups all-purpose flour

1 tablespoon confectioners' sugar

6 tablespoons unsalted butter, cold,
    cut into bits

2 tablespoons vegetable shortening

FOR THE FILLING

4 Gala or Golden Delicious apples, peeled,
    cored, and thinly sliced

2 teaspoons freshly squeezed lemon juice

¼ cup sugar

3 tablespoons unsalted butter, cut into bits

1 egg yolk

1 tablespoon granulated sugar

¼ pound Cheddar cheese, crumbled

Freshly ground black pepper (optional)

*Apples and Cheddar cheese go together so well. Perhaps it is the sweetly sharp flavors of both, a pairing made more delicious because of their contrasting textures. Come Christmas, it's too late to nibble the two side by side on the back porch, your pocket knife busy at work. But you can enjoy those flavors in a dessert that is ideal for a kitchen lunch or a fireside dinner. Crisp but sweet Gala or Golden Delicious apples are best for this rustic tart. The cheese is added as a topping after the tart has baked.*

1. In a food processor fitted with a steel blade, combine the flour, confectioners' sugar, butter, and shortening, and pulse until the mixture resembles coarse meal. Add 3 tablespoons of ice water and pulse for a few seconds more. (If the mixture is very dry, add more water and pulse until the mixture just starts to hold together.) Transfer the dough to a work surface, form it into a ball, and chill, wrapped in plastic, for 1 hour.

2. In a bowl, toss the apples, lemon juice, and sugar to combine.

3. Preheat the oven to 400°F. Line a baking sheet with parchment paper.

4. On a lightly floured surface, roll the dough into a 12-inch circle and transfer it to the baking sheet. Arrange the apple slices on the dough, leaving a 2-inch border, and dot the apples evenly with bits of butter. Fold the dough up over the edge, brush it with beaten egg yolk, and sprinkle with the granulated sugar. Bake for 30 to 35 minutes, or until the dough is lightly browned and the apples are tender.

5. Transfer the tart to a serving plate and top it with the crumbled Cheddar cheese and a grinding of fresh pepper, if desired. Serve warm.

# ✣ m a d e i r a   c a k e ✣

YIELD: 1 CAKE

FOR THE BATTER

½ cup (2 sticks) unsalted butter, softened

1 cup sugar

4 large eggs, lightly beaten

1½ cups all-purpose flour

⅓ cup finely ground blanched almonds

1 teaspoon baking powder

1 teaspoon grated lemon peel

2 tablespoons granulated sugar

FOR THE CANDIED ORANGE PEEL

½ cup sugar

Peel from one orange, cut into long, thin strips

*Akin to a simple pound cake, this English favorite gets its name from the tradition of serving it with a glass of Madeira. With its jewel-like crown of candied orange peel, this version is worthy of a Christmas toast.*

1. Preheat the oven to 325°F. Butter a Bundt pan thoroughly.

2. In the bowl of an electric mixer, beat the butter with the sugar until light and fluffy. In a heatproof bowl set over a pan of simmering water, or in the top of a double boiler set over simmering water, whisk the eggs for 2 to 3 minutes, or until warm. With the mixer running, add the eggs to the sugar mixture a little at a time and mix until well combined.

3. Into a bowl, sift the flour, ground almonds, and baking powder. Fold the dry ingredients into the egg mixture a little at a time until just combined, then fold in the lemon peel. Pour the batter into the pan and bake for 1 hour, or until a cake tester inserted in the center comes out clean. Let the cake cool in the pan for 5 minutes, then invert it onto a rack to cool completely. Sprinkle the cake with granulated sugar while it is still warm.

4. Make the candied orange peel: In a saucepan, combine 1 cup water and the sugar, bring to a boil, stirring, and simmer until the sugar is dissolved. Add the orange peel and boil for 5 minutes. Drain the peel and let cool. When the cake is cool, arrange the candied peel on top and serve.

# ✢ molasses crinkles ✢

YIELD: ABOUT 2 DOZEN COOKIES

1 cup firmly packed dark-brown sugar

½ cup (2 sticks) unsalted butter, softened

½ cup shortening

¼ cup molasses

1 large egg

2½ cups all-purpose flour

2 teaspoons baking soda

1 teaspoon cinnamon

1 teaspoon ground ginger

½ teaspoon ground clove

¼ teaspoon salt

1 cup granulated sugar for coating cookies,
    or to taste

*Though made from the thick, dense syrup that has come to signify slowness, these cookies are so good they tend to disappear from serving plates with alarming speed. A granulated-sugar coating gives them a subtle sparkle. Their aroma? Pure Christmas.*

1. In the bowl of an electric mixer, beat together the brown sugar, butter, and shortening until light and fluffy. With the mixer running, add the molasses and the egg, a little at a time, until well combined. Into a bowl, sift the flour, baking soda, cinnamon, ginger, clove, and salt. Add the dry ingredients to the sugar mixture a little at a time until well combined. Wrap the dough in plastic and chill for 1 hour.

2. Preheat the oven to 375°F. Pinch off tablespoon-size pieces of the dough and form into 1-inch balls. In a shallow bowl, roll the balls in granulated sugar until completely coated and transfer to an ungreased baking sheet. Bake for 10 to 12 minutes, or until set. Transfer the cookies to racks to cool.

# ✤ g i n g e r - l i m e   c o o k i e s ✤

YIELD: ABOUT 2 DOZEN COOKIES

2 cups all-purpose flour

1/4 cup yellow cornmeal

1 teaspoon baking soda

1 teaspoon ground ginger

1/2 teaspoon cream of tartar

1/2 teaspoon salt

6 tablespoons unsalted butter, softened

6 tablespoons vegetable shortening, chilled

1 1/3 cups, plus 2 tablespoons sugar

2 tablespoons light corn syrup

1 large egg, lightly beaten

1 teaspoon vanilla

3 tablespoons, plus 1/2 teaspoon grated lime peel (about 3 to 4 limes)

*The addition of cornmeal gives these buttery, gingery cookies an extra bit crumbliness. Lots of grated lime peel gives them zing and offers a bright, sophisticated change from the lemon flavor you'd expect to find in this kind of cookie.*

1. In a bowl, whisk the flour, cornmeal, baking soda, ginger, cream of tartar, and salt.

2. In the bowl of an electric mixer, beat together the butter, shortening, and 1 cup of the sugar until the mixture is light and fluffy. Beat in the corn syrup, egg, vanilla, and 3 tablespoons of the lime peel until combined well. With the mixer on low, add the flour and cornmeal mixture a little at a time and beat until just combined. Chill, wrapped in plastic, for 1 hour.

3. Preheat the oven to 350°F.

4. Spread 1/3 cup sugar on a plate. In a small bowl, combine the remaining 2 tablespoons sugar and 1/2 teaspoon lime peel.

5. Lightly grease a cookie sheet. Pinch off tablespoon-size pieces of dough and form into balls. Roll the balls in the plain sugar and arrange them 2 inches apart on the cookie sheet. Gently press the tops of the balls with the bottom of a glass to form rounds about 1/4 inch thick. Bake for 12 to 15 minutes, or until the edges are golden brown. While the cookies are still warm, sprinkle with the lime-and-sugar mixture and let them cool on the baking sheet for 5 minutes, then transfer them to racks to cool completely.

# ❖ bourbon-currant cookies ❖

1/3 cup bourbon whiskey

1/2 cup dried currants

1 1/2 cups (3 sticks) unsalted butter, softened

1 cup sugar

1 large egg, lightly beaten

3 cups sifted flour

Egg wash made by beating 1 large egg
   with 4 tablespoons milk

*If you think that cookies are designed for kids, think again. With bourbon whiskey in the dough, these delectable little squares are for adults only. Stack them high on a platter or cake stand for a Yuletide fête, but be sure to save enough to enjoy with a pot of tea when the party's over. It's a sweet twist on the nightcap.*

1. In a small saucepan, warm the bourbon. Remove the pan from the heat, add the currants, and let stand for 10 minutes, or until the currants are plump.

2. In the bowl of an electric mixer, beat the butter and sugar until the mixture is light and fluffy. Beat in the egg and flour a little at a time until combined. Add the currant mixture and stir until the dough is combined. Chill the dough, wrapped in plastic, for 1 hour.

3. Preheat the oven to 350°F.

4. Lightly grease a baking sheet. On a lightly floured surface, roll out the dough to a 1/4-inch thickness and cut it into 1-inch squares. Brush the cookies with the egg wash and transfer them to the baking sheet. Bake for 12 to 15 minutes, or until lightly golden. Let the cookies cool on the sheet for 5 minutes, then transfer them to racks to cool completely.

may joy & peace & wonder
surround you
throughout the year!

# Projects and Patterns

## ❀ r i b b o n - w r a p p e d   o r n a m e n t s ❀

*The classically shaped ornaments on pages 10 and 15 and below are made from an array of narrow ribbons and trims. Raid your remnants basket, or visit a ribbon store to choose the exact range of colors and textures you want. To make the ornaments you will need:*

**Cardboard**

**Assorted ribbons and trimmings**

**Craft glue**

**Narrow metallic cord**

**Felt in a complementary color**

**Buttons or appliqués**

1. With a photocopier, enlarge the pattern on page 136 to 125% (our ornament is about 4½ inches high, but you can adjust the size as you wish) and cut it out to make a template. Trace the template onto the cardboard, and cut out the shape. This is the ornament base.

2. On your worktable, arrange the ribbons until you are satisfied with the sequence in which they will appear. Place the thickest trims at the widest area of the shape.

3. Using the ornament base as a guide, trim each piece of ribbon so it measures about ½ inch beyond the edges of the base on either side.

4. Starting at the bottom of the base, wrap the first piece of ribbon around the ornament base and glue the ends to the back with craft glue. Continue working your way up the ornament, overlapping the edges of contiguous ribbons as you go, until you reach the top.

5. Cut a 6-inch piece of cord for the hanging loop. Glue the ends to the back of the base at the top. Let all the glue dry.

6. To make the backing, trace the paper template onto the felt and cut out the shape. Apply craft glue along the perimeter of the felt and adhere it to the back of the ornament to cover the ribbon ends.

7. Glue a button or little trinket to the front of the ornament as a finishing touch.

# ⊹ woven ribbon stocking ⊹

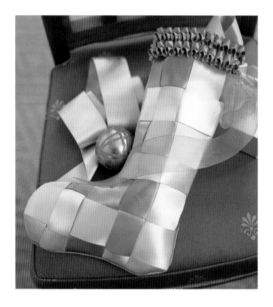

*In a blend of pale colors, the shimmering woven-ribbon stocking on page 17 and above shows off the season's palette beautifully. Solid-color ribbons in the same weave work best; we used double-faced satin ribbons of various widths, but grosgrain would also be very pretty. One, or even two, lengths of ruffled ribbon makes a stylish cuff. To make a stocking, you will need:*

**2 yards each of three or four different-color ribbons, each 1 1/2 to 2 inches wide**

**Adhesive tape**

**1/2 yard of iron-on fusing**

**1 yard of wide, fancy ribbon for the cuff**

**1/2 yard of fabric, such as satin or dupioni**

**Sewing supplies**

1. With a photocopier, enlarge the pattern on page 136 to 200% (or adjust it to the size you wish) and cut it out to make a template. Place the template on a hard, level work surface.

2. Start by laying lengths of ribbon vertically over the pattern. Place each ribbon right next to the other and cover the pattern from edge to edge. (Be sure to place one-sided ribbon right-side down.) Cut the ends of each ribbon about 2 inches beyond the pattern. Tape the ribbon ends to your work surface to hold them in place.

3. Repeat Step 2, working horizontally. Remove the stocking template from underneath the ribbons. Starting from the top, weave the ribbons over and under one another, alternating the weave in each row.

4. Cut a piece of fusing to fit the ribbon rectangle, place it on top, and fuse it to the ribbons with an iron set at medium high. Use a pressing motion with the iron, and check the ribbon and fusing every so often to make sure they are bonding. If using a lightweight backing fabric, you might want to add a layer of fusing to the wrong side of the backing.

5. Place the right sides of the ribbon and the backing fabrics together, and pin the template to the fabrics. Cut out both panels.

6. Leaving a 1/4-inch seam allowance, sew a seam around the perimeter of the stocking, leaving the cuff open.

7. So the seams will lie smoothly, clip notches in the seam allowance at the curved edges, to about 1/16 inch from the seam. Turn the stocking right-side out and press flat with a medium-hot iron.

8. Finish the cuff: Turn down the fabric 1/4 inch into the stocking, press, and repeat. Sew a hem all the way around the cuff. To add the ruffle, cut a piece of fancy ribbon about 1 inch longer than the circumference of the stocking top. Tuck the edges under where they meet at the back, and hand-stitch the ribbon to the stocking. You could add a second layer of ribbon to the cuff, depending on your design.

9. To create a loop for hanging, cut a 6 1/2-inch length of ribbon and form a loop. Stitch both ends to the inside back of the cuff area so a 3-inch loop extends from the stocking.

# cinch-top favor cones

*These versatile gift cones— page 34 and below— are modeled after Victorian treat containers from long ago, with a nod toward the ice cream cone as well. But instead of ice cream, these cones should get filled with handfuls of candies or little trinkets to give to guests at a party. They could also hang on the tree or be wired into garlands. To make one cone, you will need:*

**½ yard heavyweight patterned wrapping paper**

**Stapler**

**20-by-5½-inch piece of colored crepe paper**

**Craft glue or hot-glue gun**

**Trim (tinsel garland or crepe-paper ruffle)**

**18 inches of ¼-inch-wide ribbon**

1. With a photocopier, enlarge the cone pattern on page 136 to 200% (or adjust it to the size you wish) and cut the pattern out. Trace this pattern onto the back side of the wrapping paper, and cut out the shape.

2. Roll the wrapping paper piece into a cone shape, overlapping as indicated on the pattern, and staple once through the seam about 2 inches down from the top edge to secure. Trim the top of the cone with scissors to even it out. Once you are pleased with the shape, staple the seam twice more about ¾ inch apart.

3. To make the cinched top of the cone, roll the piece of crepe paper into a cylinder, matching the circumference of the top of the cone. Check your cylinder against the inside of the cone, and when the size is right, secure the layers with three evenly spaced staples around the edge of one end of the crepe-paper cylinder.

4. Apply craft glue or hot glue around the circumference of the stapled end of the cylinder, and carefully position the cylinder about ½ inch inside the cone. The seam of the crepe paper should meet the seam of the cone. Insert your hand into the cone and press the papers together to make a secure seal. Let dry.

5. Cut a length of tinsel garland or crepe-paper ruffle long enough to encircle the outside top edge of the cone. Apply dabs of craft glue or hot glue all the way around the outside top edge of the cone. Starting at the cone seam, wrap the trim around the edge until it meets the other end. Press gently to hold it in place. Let the glue dry.

6. Fill your cone with whatever treats you like, then cinch the top and tie it with the length of ribbon. You can trim the top of the crepe paper for a neater edge. For a fuller dome at the top, insert a poof of crumpled tissue before cinching the crepe paper.

# ✤ g l i t t e r e d   g o o d i e   b o x e s ✤

*Transform containers from ice cream or yogurt into sparkly packages— page 35 and above. Of course, if you prefer, you can purchase new containers for this project. Gather some vintage cards or illustrations to embellish the boxes (make color photocopies if you don't want to use your originals). This is a messy project, so cover your work-table with newspaper. To make the boxes, you will need:*

**Vintage images from postcards, greeting cards, or calling cards**

**½ yard double-sided adhesive paper, such as Twin-Tac**

**Clean, dry containers in assorted sizes**

**Spray glue**

**Glitter in assorted colors and in matte white**

**Tinsel or metallic cording or trims**

**Clear-drying craft glue**

1. Prepare the label: Choose an image and cut it to size for the container you wish to decorate. Using the image as a template, trace around its edges onto the back of the double-sided adhesive paper. Cut out the adhesive paper and peel away one side of the backing; adhere the paper to the front of the container, leaving the backing on the other side.

2. Working in sections, spray the container with spray glue and sprinkle it liberally with glitter. Continue working your way around the container, covering the whole thing except for the area of adhesive paper. Make sure to leave a tiny section near the edge of the adhesive paper glitter-free so you will be able to find and peel off the backing.

3. Let the first coat of glitter dry, then repeat the process until the container is completely covered.

4. Prepare the lid in the same way as the container, spraying it with glue and covering it with glitter. Once the lid is dry, use craft glue to add tinsel trim or metallic cord around the edge of the lid.

5. If you like, you can glue on some tinsel trim to the back edges of your image before you adhere it to the container. Then peel away the remaining backing from the adhesive paper and position your label on this area. If you're using the containers for edible gifts, be sure to wrap the food in tissue or other paper to protect it from picking up glitter.

# ❊ "d r e s d e n"   f a v o r   c u p s ❊

*Inspired by the molded paper ornaments first made in and around Dresden, Germany, in the nineteenth century, these favor cups — page 52 and below — can be used to hold all manner of treats: nuts, candies, tiny treasures. Put one at each place setting or hang them by their handles on the branches of a tabletop tree near the door for guests to take as they depart. To make the cups, you will need:*

**Small seedling peat pots**

**Acrylic paint in the color of your choice**

**Sponge paintbrush**

**Vintage images from postcards, greeting cards, or clip art**

**Clear acrylic spray sealant**

**Craft glue**

**Glitter**

**Piercing tool, such as a large-eyed sewing needle or a compass point**

**Fine-gauge wire**

**1.** Paint both the outside and the inside of the pot with two coats of acrylic paint. Let dry.

**2.** Cut your vintage image to size (photocopy the image if you don't wish to use the original). Apply glue to the back of the image and press into place on the cup. Let dry.

**3.** Spray the outside and inside of the cup with clear acrylic sealant. Let dry.

**4.** Apply craft glue to the rim of the cup and coat with glitter. Let dry.

**5.** Pierce two small holes on the opposite sides of the cup about 1/4 inch from the edge. Cut a piece of wire about 8 inches long for the handle. Insert the ends of the wire through the holes in the cup and twist the ends to hold them in place.

# ✤ w a l l p a p e r e d   a l b u m ✤

*Plain photo albums or journals turn into gorgeous gifts—page 53 and below—with the simple addition of pretty paper and trimmings. Durable wallpaper is an excellent choice for books that will be handled often. You can use leftover wallpaper from your own home decorating projects, or check with your local design store to see if they are disposing of any large-size sample books. The book shown has separate front and back wooden covers that we coated individually with toile wallpaper and then threaded through with ribbon, but any book you choose will work just as well. To make a covered book, you will need:*

**Book or photo album with a sturdy cardboard or wood cover**

**1 yard wallpaper or other heavyweight decorative paper**

**Spray glue**

**Clear drying craft glue**

**Vintage image, alphabet stickers, or rubber stamps and ink**

**Ribbon or trims as desired**

1. Open the book and lay the covers against the back side of the wallpaper. Using a ruler, measure about ½ to 1 inch beyond the edges of the covers onto the paper and mark with a pencil.

2. Cut out the paper and apply spray glue to the back side. Center the covers of the open book over the glue-coated paper, so the extra border of paper is evenly spaced around the cover edges. Press the covers and spine into place on the paper.

3. Wrap the excess paper around to the insides of the covers and secure with craft glue. At each corner, fold the paper into a mitered shape (in the same way as you would wrap a gift).

4. For a clean finish for the insides of the covers, measure and cut end papers to size from the leftover wallpaper, making sure it covers the flaps wrapped around from the front. Spray-glue and press into place.

5. Use your imagination to decorate the album. Cut out a piece of card stock and imprint a message with rubber stamps or stickers. Select a vintage holiday image (photocopy the image if you don't want to use the original) to apply to the cover. Incorporate ribbons, trims, buttons, beads, or tiny treasures. Adhere any decorations to the front cover of the album with craft glue. If you like, you can cut a piece of ribbon in a coordinating color and tie it around the album.

# ✣ l a c e - u p  s k a t e  i n v i t a t i o n s ✣

*Our handmade skating party invitations⏤ page 63 and below⏤ become charming keepsakes when the day is over. We like to make them with sparkly white card stock, but you can choose whatever paper you wish or even create skates and ribbon laces in an array of colors. To make the invitations, you will need:*

**Card stock**

**Silver-colored card stock**

**¼-inch hole punch**

**¼-inch-wide ribbon**

**Glue stick**

**Snowflake stickers or adhesive dots**

1. With a photocopier, enlarge the skate and blade patterns on page 137 to 200% (or adjust it to the size you wish) and cut them out.

2. Fold a sheet of card stock in half. Place the top of the skate pattern along the fold and trace around its edges with a pencil. Cut out the skate shape through both layers of the cardboard, leaving the two panels attached at the fold.

3. Trace the blade pattern on the silver-colored card stock and cut it out.

4. With a pencil, mark a series of four lacing holes, as indicated on the pattern, along the edge of the top skate. Punch out the holes.

5. Cut a piece of ribbon or cording 8 inches long to make the "laces." Open the card and secure one end of the ribbon inside the cover skate with a snowflake sticker or adhesive dot near the bottom lacing hole. Wrap the lace around to the front of the card and begin to thread it through the holes. At the top of the skate, tie a bow from the excess lacing.

6. Using the glue stick, adhere the blade to the inside bottom of the top skate shape.

7. If you like, decorate the front of the invitation with snowflake stickers or adhesive dots placed at the ankle, heel, and toe.

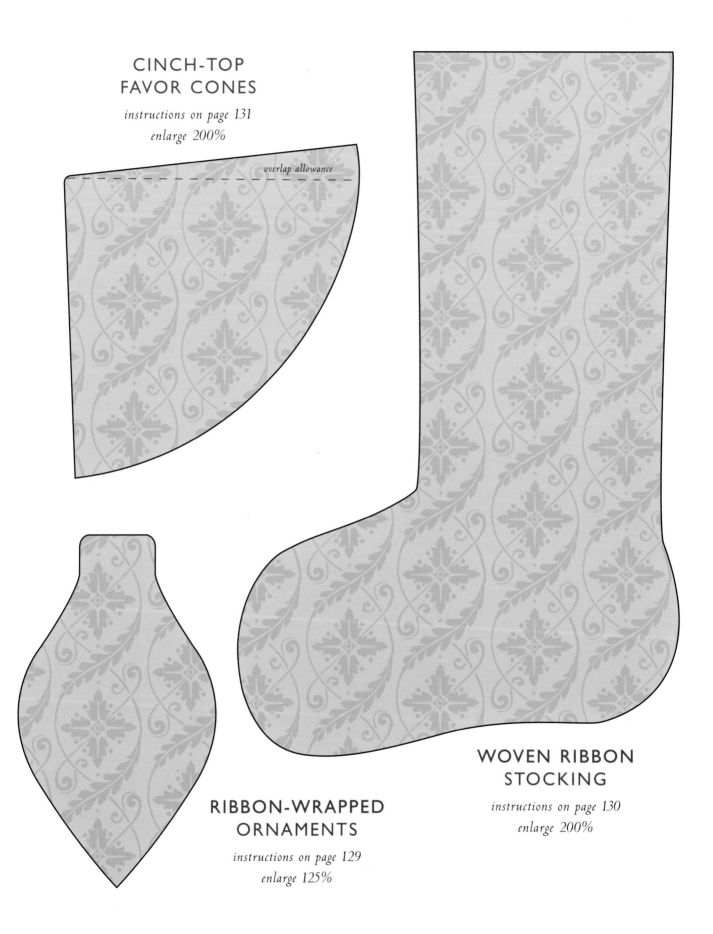

## CINCH-TOP
## FAVOR CONES

*instructions on page 131*
*enlarge 200%*

overlap allowance

## RIBBON-WRAPPED
## ORNAMENTS

*instructions on page 129*
*enlarge 125%*

## WOVEN RIBBON
## STOCKING

*instructions on page 130*
*enlarge 200%*

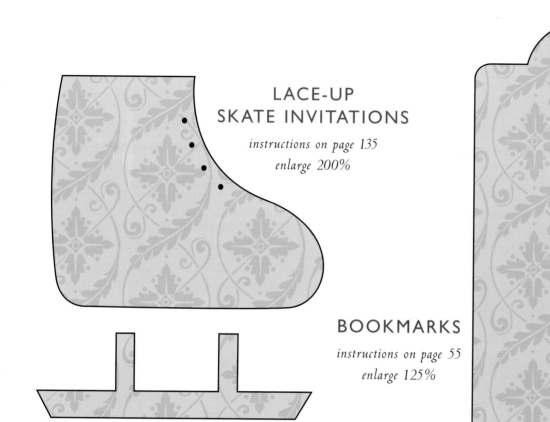

# LACE-UP
# SKATE INVITATIONS

*instructions on page 135*
*enlarge 200%*

# BOOKMARKS

*instructions on page 55*
*enlarge 125%*

# SILHOUETTE STATIONERY

*instructions on page 57*
*actual size*

# Resources

## WINTER'S COLORS

**pages 10–15**
*Ribbons* from Ribbon Connection, 2971 Tea Garden Street, San Leandro, CA 64577; (510) 614-1825.

**page 10**
*Small silk stockings* from Denise Fiedler of Bravura, at the Loom Co., 31 West 27th Street, Tenth Floor, New York, NY 10001; (212) 889-1182.

*Hand-blown glass ornaments* from Gilmor Glassworks, P.O. Box 961, Millerton, NY 12546; (888) 256-4527.

*Handmade cards* from J. Stone Cards, 1 J. Stone Plaza, Silverton, OR 97381; (800) 525-4813 or www.jstonecards.com.

*Gift wrap* from Glitterwrap, 701 Ford Road, Rockaway, NJ 07866; (800) 745-4883.

*Bandboxes* from Hannah's Treasures, 947 Oak Road, Harlan, IA 51537; (712) 755-3173 or www.hannahstreasures.com.

*Garden chair* from Bago Luma, (830) 249-2499.

*"Fiesole" fabric used as tree skirt* from Designers Guild at Osbourne & Little, (212) 751-3333. To the trade.

*Lavender and blue candles* from Barrick Design, Inc., 541 North Mulberry Street, Lancaster, PA 17603; (717) 295-4800.

*Cookies* from Old River Road, (530) 342-1517.

**page 11**
*Hand-blown glass ornament* from Gilmor Glassworks, see above.

**page 13**
*Garden chair* from Bago Luma, see above.

*"Saville" wool fabric on seat* from Osborne & Little, see above.

*Bandboxes* from Hannah's Treasures, see above.

*Mesh drawstring pouches and nesting boxes* from Joneses International, (800) 566-3770 or www.packageit.net.

*Blue candle* from Barrick Design, Inc., see above.

*Cookies* from Old River Road, see above.

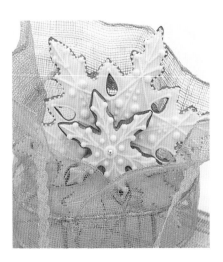

**page 15 (right)**
*Bandbox* from Hannah's Treasures, see above.

**page 16**
*Ribbon* from Mokuba, 55 West 39th Street, New York, NY 10018; (212) 869-8900.

**page 17**

*Ribbon for stocking* from Mokuba, see above.

*Sparkly paper* from Kate's Paperie, (888) 941-9196 or www.katespaperie.com.

**pages 18, 19**

*Large spinning top and silver cone glass ornaments* from Villeroy & Boch, (800) 845-5376 or www.villeroyboch.com.

*Ribbons* from Mokuba, see above.

**page 21**

*Napkin* from Traditions by Pamela Kline, 29 Route 9H, Claverack, NY 12513; (518) 851-3975 or www.traditionspamelakline.com.

**page 23**

*Sheer striped paper* from Kate's Paperie, see above.

# Joyful Wrappings

**pages 24, 25**

*Cone stars* from Every Day's a Holiday, (415) 776-2076.

*Paper on boxes* from Flax, (800) 622-6213 or www.flaxart.com.

*Polka-dot paper and tinsel garland* from Addison Endpapers, 6397 Telegraph Avenue, Oakland, CA 94609; (510) 601-8112.

*Louis XVI-style "Perle" chair* from Nest, (415) 292-6198.

**page 26**

*Beaded ornaments* from Garnet Hill, (800) 622-6213 or www.garnethill.com.

**page 27**

*Ribbon* from the Tail of the Yak, 2632 Ashby Avenue, Berkeley, CA 94705; (510) 841-9891.

*Papers* from Flax, see above.

*Paper flowers and card* from Addison Endpapers, see above.

**page 28**

*Silver paper on small box* from Every Day's a Holiday, see above.

*Ribbon* from Hyman Hendler, 67 West 38th Street, New York, NY 10018; (212) 840-8393.

*Diamond-patterned paper* from Addison Endpapers, see above.

**page 29**

*Papers* from Flax, see above.

*Yellow and bright pink ribbons* from Satin Moon, available at Flax, see above.

*Porcelain tumbler and green satin ribbon* from Tail of the Yak, see above.

*Metallic pressed-paper daisies, green soutache, and pink ribbon* from Addison Endpapers, see above.

**page 30**

*Papers* from Flax, see above.

*Ribbon* from Hyman Hendler, see above.

*Cushion* from Nest, see above.

**page 31**

*Papers and paper flowers* from Addison Endpapers, see above.

*Green ribbon* from Tail of the Yak, see above.

*Pink ribbon* from Satin Moon, available at Flax, see above.

**pages 33–35**

*Ribbons* from Mokuba, 55 West 39th Street, New York, NY 10018; (212) 869-8900.

**page 34**

*Polka-dot paper and crepe paper* from Kate's Paperie, (888) 941-9196 or www.katespaperie.com.

**pages 36, 37**

*"Shenandoah" table runner and tablecloth fabric, "Provençal Ball Fringe" table runner and curtain-tie trim, and "Wellfleet Ticking" curtain lining* from Schumacher, (800) 988-7775. To the trade.

*"Rose Botanique" curtain fabric* from Amy Karyn, (215) 297-9703.

*"Fika" double-pedestal tea-table and "Gripsholm" love seat covered in "Cavalier Check"* from Country Swedish, (212) 838-1976. To the trade.

*Hartley Greens creamware and vintage transferware* from Tabletop Designs by Stephanie Queller, (631) 283-1313.

*"Duchessa" trim for napkin tie* from Scalamandré, (800) 932-4361. To the trade.

*Napkins* from Tabletop Designs by Stephanie Queller, see above.

*Leafy metal plate holders* from Groundwork, at Relish, (404) 355-3735.

**page 38 (bottom)**

*Ribbon for napkin cuff* from Mokuba, see above.

**page 39**

*French washed-linen tablecloth with hem-stitched edge* from Rural Residence, 316 Warren Street, Hudson, NY, 12534; (518) 822-1061 or www.ruralresidence.com.

*Ribbon for tablecloth* from Mokuba, see above.

# NATURE COMES INDOORS

**page 40**

*"Fabergé Santa" ornaments* from Patricia Breen, (702) 585-5800 or www.patriciabreen.com.

**page 43**

*"Fabergé Santa" ornaments* from Patricia Breen, see above.

**pages 44, 45**

*Plants* from Hollandia Nurseries, 103 Old Hawleyville Road, Bethel, CT 06801; (203) 743-0267 or www.hollandianurseryct.com, and from Walnut Hill Greenhouses, Litchfield, CT, (860) 482-5832.

*Ornaments* from Focal Point, 36 Bank Street, New Milford, CT 06776; (860) 355-0081.

*Glazed pots* from Potluck Studios, 23 Main Street, Accord, NY 12404; (845) 626-2300.

# PAPER GREETINGS

**page 53**

*Thiebault Toile Resource Collection wallpaper (pattern #839-T-9557)* available at Janovic, 215 Seventh Avenue, New York, NY 10013; (212) 645-5454 or www.janovic.com.

*Ribbon* from Mokuba, 55 West 39th Street, New York, NY 10018; (212) 869-8900.

**pages 54, 55**

*Papers* from Kate's Paperie, (888) 941-9196 or www.katespaperie.com.

*Ribbon* from Mokuba, see above.

**page 56**

*Papers* from Kate's Paperie, see above

*Narrow striped ribbon* from Mokuba, see above.

*Vintage metallic ribbon* from Tinsel Trading Co., 47 West 38th Street, New York, NY 10018; (212) 730-1030.

**page 57**

*Antique Wedgwood vase* from Bardith, 901 Madison Avenue, New York, NY, 10021; (212) 737-3775.

**page 58**

*Papers* from Kate's Paperie, see above.

**page 59**

*Wide brown moiré ribbon* from Tinsel Trading Co., see above.

# A SKATING PARTY

**page 60–68**

*Sweaters* from Tipperary at Tara, Ltd., 3956 NY2 Brunswick Road, Troy, NY 12180; (800) 255-8272 or www.tipperarytrading.com, and from N. Peale, 5 West 5th Street, New York, NY 10019; (800) 962-5541.

*Hats* from Portolano, 32 West 39th Street, Fifth Floor, New York, NY 10018; (212) 719-4403 or www.portolano.com, and from Fisherman Out of Ireland, 011-353-73-382-22.

*Gloves and scarves* from Portolano, see above, and from Brooklyn Handknit, (212) 594-4999 or www.brooklynhandknit.com, available at Spacial Etc., 199 Bedford Avenue, Brooklyn, NY 11211; (718) 599-7962.

**page 63**

*Ribbons* from Mokuba, 55 West 39th Street, New York, NY 10018; (212) 869-8900.

*Paper* from Kate's Paperie, (888) 941-9196 or www.katespaperie.com.

**page 65**

*White bowl* from Match, Inc., (201) 792-9444.

**page 69**

*Silvered paper* from Kate's Paperie, see above.

# SWEET PRESENTS

**page 70**

*Gift tin and faux wax seal* from Kate's Paperie, (888) 941-9196 or www.katespaperie.com.

*Ribbon* from Mokuba, 55 West 39th Street, New York, NY 10018; (212) 869-8900.

**page 71**

*Organdy ribbon* from Midori, (800) 659-3049.

**page 73**

*Silver corrugated boxes* from Surprise Packages/Specialty Boxes, available through Dessert Delivery, (212) 838-5411.

*Ribbon* from Midori, see above.

*Blue paper in background* from Kate's Paperie, see above.

**page 74**

*Monogrammed box and paper doily* from Williams-Sonoma, (800) 541-1262 or www.williams-sonoma.com.

**page 76**

*Cake box* from Loose Ends, 2065 Madrona Avenue SE, Salem, OR 97302; (503) 390-2348 or www.looseends.com.

*Green ribbon* from Midori, see above.

**page 78**

*"Baroque angel with lute" cookie mold* from House-on-the-Hill, (630) 969-2624 or www.houseonthehill.net.

*Bell jar* from Abigail's, (800) 678-8485.

*Layer of spun metal* from Loose Ends, see above.

*Gold paper in background* from Kate's Paperie, see above.

*Ribbons* from Renaissance Ribbons, available at Kate's Paperie, see above.

**page 79**

*Old-fashioned shortbread jar* from English Country Antiques, (631) 537-0606.

*Vintage silver cake server* from
Tabletop Designs, (631) 283-1313.

*Ribbon* from Midori, see above.

**page 80**

*Julep cups* from the Beauchamp
Collection, (800) 469-0564 or
www.beauchampcollection.com.

*Tin-leaf garland* from Loose Ends,
see above.

**page 81**

*Round box and pinecones* from
Loose Ends, see above.

*Blue twine* from Raffit Ribbons,
(877) 723-3487 or www.raffit.com.

**page 83**

*Paper on jars and twine* from
Kate's Paperie, see above.

*Three-tier cake stand* from Relish,
(404) 355-3735.

*Antiqued gilded fruit* from
Loose Ends, see above.

# HOLIDAY
# ENTERTAINING

**page 84**

*Silver punch bowl and ice bucket* from
Pottery Barn, (888) 779-5176
or www.potterybarn.com.

*Glass cylinders with candles* from IKEA,
(800) 434-4532 or www.ikea.com.

**pages 86, 87**

*Floral arrangement* by Jack Folmer for
Very Special Flowers, New York, NY,
(212) 206-7236.

**page 89 (top)**

*Golden-brown platter* from Banana
Republic, (888) 277-8953 or
www.bananarepublic.com.

**page 89 (bottom)**

*Pewter "Pietro" tray* from Tuscan Square,
16 West 51st Street, New York, NY
10020; (212) 977-7777.

**page 91**

*Turkey platter* from The Country
Dining Room Antiques,
178 Main Street, Great Barrington,
MA 01230; (413) 528-5050
or www.countrydiningroomantiq.com.

*Saltcellar and square-based glasses* from
William Yeoward, (800) 818-8484,
www.williamyeowardcrystal.com.

*Faceted glasses* from Rural Residence,
316 Warren Street, Hudson,
NY 12534; (518) 822-1061 or
www.ruralresidence.com.

**page 93 (top)**

*Light blue plate* from Dansk,
(800) 293-2675 or www.dansk.com.

**page 93 (bottom)**

*Antique English china* from Bardith,
901 Madison Avenue, New York,
NY 10021; (212) 737-3775.

**page 95**

*Antique English china* from Bardith,
see above.

# Photography Credits

**John Bessler**
page 82

**Guy Bouchet**
page 20 (left)

**Christopher Drake**
front cover; pages 40, 42, 43, 141 (left)

**Richard Felber**
page 141 (right)

**Steve Gross & Sue Daly**
page 8

**Charles Maraia**
pages 7 (third from top), 71–81, 83, 96, 143 (left); back cover (top left, bottom right)

**Jeff McNamara**
pages 88, 89 (top)

**Susan Gentry McWhinney**
pages 1, 2, 6, 7 (top, second from top), 10–19, 20 (right), 22, 23, 26, 32–35, 38, 39, 41, 46 (bottom), 47, 51–59, 63, 69, 70, 129–135, 139; back cover (top center, top right, middle left, bottom left, bottom center)

**Minh & Wass**
page 93 (top)

**Toshi Otsuki**
pages 36, 37, 60–62, 64–68, 138, 142

**David Prince**
pages 5, 21, 44, 45, 46 (top), 50

**Laura Resen**
pages 84, 86, 87, 143 (right)

**Christina Schmidhofer**
pages 3, 24, 25, 27–31, 138, 144

**Ellen Silverman**
pages 89 (bottom), 93 (bottom), 94, 95

**Michael Skott**
page 140

**William P. Steele**
pages 48, 49, 85

**Ann Stratton**
pages 7 (bottom), 90–92